I couoldn't see the words for the threes.

I wouold get very embarbarrassed.

If I was toed to read a prick at school, I felt a rihgt page. TreueueelY!

But, thank Bog! At last I am competely cuered! And it is all bicarb of one mam. MEL SHIT,

Whey the opporpotamus of this bonk came up it was Mel Shit who staid I shouould wrote it on my owl.

I was scarred.

'A hole bonk! On my *owl*!'

'You can do it', he staid. 'You have wanked hard. You are wroting like norbal peephole.'

'Trueueueuly?

'Wouould I lice to you?'

Let me tell you. Whey he staid that, their were teirs in my ayes.

And now with Rory McGrasp and Clit Andrexson I have wristen this bonk.

It has been a lemur of love.

Thank you.
And thank you, Mel Shit.

Griff Rhys Jabberwocky.

Mon Repos,
Chiswick

Dear Mr. Rhys Jones,

In reply to your letter of the fifteenth inst., I am writing on behalf of Mr. Smith who has passed this matter on to me.

If you wish to proceed with this book may I make it quite clear that Mr. Smith does not wish it to be published. He will not write any part of it. He will not contribute any ideas towards it. He will not attend any photographic sessions in order to have "Silly" or frivolous photographs taken for it.

He will not appear on Terry Wogan's programme on the BBC and manage to slip in several gratuitous "plugs" for it.

He will not read it. He will not idly thumb through it. He will not leave it lying ostentatiously around when he has "people in."

He will not give free copies of it to his friends and relations at Christmas.

He will not walk into bookshops and cunningly sneak it to the top of a pile of other humorous publications.

He will not fervently scan "The Sunday Times" Bestsellers lists before going to church.

He will not attend parties in a tweed jacket with leather patches on the elbows wearing old-fashioned glasses and sit by himself in a corner.

He will not ring the publishers because his local W. H. Smith's does not have a seven-foot display in the window.

His heart will not miss a beat and his stomach will not churn when he sees vast heaps of the book remaindered in a disused shoe shop in the Kilburn High Road.

He will not sob bitterly when "The Observer" calls it a load of codswallop.

In return for these undertakings he will, of course, expect his usual advance and a percentage of the gross to be not less than 83 per cent.

Yours faithfully,

L. Lee. (P.A. to Mr. Smith)

P.S.
Mr. Smith has asked me to remind you that the original terms of your contract with him have not lapsed. The car has not been cleaned for at least three weeks now. Please attend to this matter at your earliest convenience.

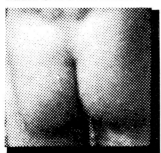
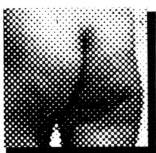

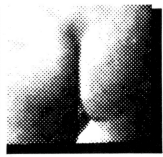

10 THINGS YOU *NEVER* KNEW ABOUT SAMANTHA FOX

1 *She is highly intelligent.*

2 *She is rather shy and retiring.*

3 *Her ambition is to be a nun.*

4 *Her father is not interested in money.*

5 *She is 5' 11" tall.*

6 *She is NOT a dumb blonde (it's bleached).*

7 *To make her breasts, Madame Tussauds had to melt down Laurel AND Hardy.*

8 *She is studying Nuclear Physics with the Open University.*

9 *Had she lived in the age of Charles II, she would be dead by now.*

10 *Without clothes, her body looks like this. (All right, you DID know that – but at least it's fairly true.)*

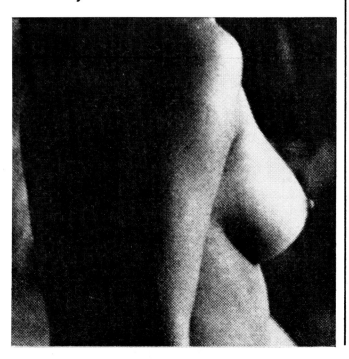

NEW STYLE O.S. MAP

This is a section taken from one of the new Ordnance Survey maps (soon to be introduced), excluding many of the boring symbols like 'Ancient Monument' and 'Level Crossing Without Gates' and replacing them with more interesting ones.

M	Massage parlour
M	Massage parlour with extra personal services
	Orchard (or very large cribbage board)
	Public telephone
	Public toilet
	Indian takeaway
	Chinese takeaway
	Cattery (or could be two Chinese takeaways next to each other, if you don't get your cat back it is)
	Fly squashed on map
	Private hospital
	NHS hospital
	Airport
	Airport with above average of Boeing 737's landing
	Church without spire
	Church without congregation
	Lake
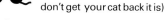	Motorway
	Wet motorway
	Information centre
	Information centre for people who don't want to know anything
	Mountain refuge hut
	Parking
	Parking on mountain refuge hut only
	Bridge
	Footbridge
	Lock
	Dam
	Bollocks!
	Caravan site
	Cheap caravan site

Jerry BUILDERS

"Rome wasn't built in a day."
Stan Jerry

"It would have been only we was waiting for the undercoat to dry."
Ron Jerry

Dear Jerry Bros,
I think I have damp in my walls. What should I do?
Yours
Fred Watkins

Dear. Oh dear,
Oh dear oh dear oh dear oh dear. Tut tut tut. How long have you lived here then? Blimey. Look at that. That patch on your walls. Dear oh dear. Yes, I will have a cup of tea – thanks. Milk and eight sugars. New conversion, is it then? Yes . . . Irish what done it was it? O-o-o-o-o-oh . . . Pakis? Dear oh dear. You know what you've got, don't you. Damp. Yeah – rampant rising damp, mate. You wanna get that seen to. Lean against that wall and you'll most likely drown. Any more tea, love?
Yours
Ron

Dear Jerry Bros,
When are you going to come and finish my bloody bathroom extension that you started in 1983?
Yours
J.C. Perkins

Dear Mr Perkins,
We regret any inconvenience to you caused by the international shortage of bathroom supplies. That and the abnormally bad weather has meant delays our end, of course. With all this rain we can't start work on the walls until we've finished the roof and unfortunately we can't seem to get the roof to stay up.
If you're busting for a pony and trap, feel free to come down the yard and use ours.
Yours
Stan

Dear Jerry Bros,
What is the best way to pay a builder for a finished piece of work?
Yours
L. Richards

Dear Mr Richards,
You've actually had some work finished . . . You are a lucky man. Well, if you're VAT registered then the builder will probably charge you VAT what you can claim back later. If it's a certain sort of legit home or office premises improvement, then you can probably claim it against tax provided the builder gives you a proper receipt and bungs it through his books and all that bleedin' palaver. So . . . in short, cash. Green readies and get a move on.
I hope that answers your question.
Yours
Ron

BEFORE . . .

. . . AND AFTER

You'll be glad you employed a professional.

◀ *The wrong way to convert your front room into a garage.*

▼ *Never employ firemen to put up your scaffolding.*

Dear Jerry Bros,
          I live in an old terrace and get a lot of noise through the walls from my neighbours playing their stereo etc. Is there any way to install soundproofing or would cavity-wall insulation help?
                    Yours
                    Mrs F. Hurst

Dear Missus,
          May I recommend Noel O'Rourke & Sons of Holloway, who specialize in this sort of work. Noel will go round to your neighbours and threaten to stuff their stereo up their arse if they don't turn it down.
                    Yours
                    Stan

Dear Jerry Brothers,
          We would like to see all books and accounts for Tax Years 1955/56 and successive years to the present day.
                    Inland Revenue

Dear Inrand Levenue,
          Jelly Bluvvers no here no more. We take over. You want nice genelous portion chicken chow mein? Eh?
                    Yours
                    Dave the Chink

◀ *We can deliver the home of your dreams within hours.*

N⁰·26: A life in the day of a BLUEBOTTLE

N⁰·27: A life in the day of a MAYFLY

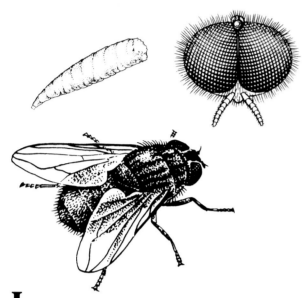

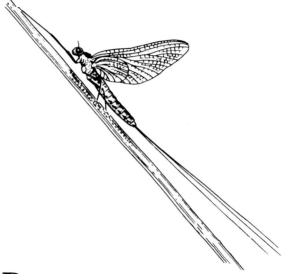

I'M VERY MUCH AN EARLY RISER. HAVING TWO bloody great wings makes getting up no problem at all. Before breakfast I usually have time to go for a few circuits of the inside of the dustbin.

Fitness is *very* important to me. Yomping around large dog turds is great for general fitness and a good anaerobic exercise is landing on a cat's ear – flying off when the cat flicks its tail and landing again, straightaway, when the tail has retreated. And so on and so on. Then it's back through the kitchen window for breakfast.

This is the only time I have an opportunity to crawl up and down the daily papers. Breakfast is usually a hurried affair, hovering over the table and jetting briefly into the sugar, toast, marmalade and any leftover bacon rind. This is all washed down with a nervous scamper round the edge of a coffee-cup.

Modern technology has spoiled breakfast for many a bluebottle – the advent of *cling-film* especially. It is invisible and acts as a trampoline. One minute you're dive-bombing a plate of sandwiches, and the next 'BOINGGG'… you're back on the ceiling.

After breakfast there's the hurly-burly of getting the kids off the cowpat. I've two million of the little blighters, so it's a time-consuming business. Last week, we had a bit of good news – my eldest has got into Oxford on a pork chop.

Then it's off to the real business of being a bluebottle – hour after hour spent circling the light-bulb, trampling around the butter-dish and banging your head on the window. Then there's a relaxing half-hour lying upside down on the ceiling.

Having it off in mid-air is surely one of the great perks of being a bluebottle. I can't think of *anyone* else who does that… except possibly air-hostesses. Recently though I haven't been getting my legs over as much as I'd like. My wife has complained of severe headaches…which is, of course, one of the drawbacks of banging your head against the window for twelve hours a day.

Night-time is, naturally, a time for sleeping. It's usually fairly easy to find a sleeping human being and fly in low over them with your extra-loud night buzz – and then disappear as soon as the light comes on and they come looking for you with a rolled-up newspaper or one of those floppy tennis-racket things.

It's a short life, but a *happy* life.

BORN. EAT. SHAG. DIE.

**EVERY ADVERTISEMENT
CARRIES A GOVERNMENT HEALTH WARNING
IN CASE YOU DON'T REALIZE IT IS
A CIGARETTE ADVERTISEMENT**

RAY OF THE RAVERS

RAY RACEY HEADS HOME TO WIN FOR MALCHESTER RAVERS, BUT LOOKS UPSET

MY PERM! IT'S RUINED MY PERM!

RAY GOES OFF WITH HAIR-STRAIN ON COMES BALDY BLACKMORE

GOOD LUCK, BLACKIE. I'M OFF TO PHONE JULIAN AT CRIMPERS.

SO... MALCHESTER RAVERS 2... OLDFIELD UNITED 1.

FANTASTIC! WHICH ONE DO I PLAY FOR?

I'M LINDA FOX... THE PAGE THREE GIRL FROM THE SUN.

I'VE NEVER READ THAT FAR.

RAY SCORES FOR THE SECOND TIME THAT DAY

LINDA SENDS OVER A COUPLE OF BOUNCERS

MONDAY MORNING TRAINING AS USUAL

BRILLIANT CONTROL ON SATURDAY, RAY. WELL DONE.

THANKS... WELL, SHE WASN'T ON THE PILL SO I HAD NO CHOICE.

STERN WORDS FROM BILL McBACKHEEL, THE MANAGER

BIG GAME SATURDAY, RAY. REMEMBER IT'S A MORNING FIXTURE.

OH. I'M SUPPOSED TO BE OPENING A SUPERMARKET.

GET YOUR PRIORITIES RIGHT, SON. OK?

SATURDAY ARRIVES...

AND SO I DECLARE THIS SUPERMARKET OPEN.

THE END

Paper 415
ENGLISH LIT
1500 – 1650

OXFORD AND CAMBRIDGE
Joint Examination Board

Wednesday 22 June
Afternoon: 3 hours

Section 1

Candidates should write on ONE *side of the paper* **only**. *Do* **not** *attempt to answer more than* ONE *question at a time.*

Do **not** SWEAT *profusely on the paper.*

Do not immediately start scribbling HUNDREDS *of pages of notes, it annoys the other candidates.*

Read the questions carefully **before** *you begin to write. Remember your* ENTIRE FUTURE LIFE, *your* CAREER PROSPECTS *and subsequent* FINANCIAL STATUS *in the world is dependent on the next* THREE *hours. Above all, do* **not** *worry. Believe you me, the hasty answer could be a* WRONG *move. I know you're anxious to get on and get something down, anything, but take it from one who knows: too much, too fast, is silly. Very, very* SILLY *indeed. I was the sort of person who knew all the answers, but for some reason I just couldn't do exams. The pressure, I suppose. Still, too late now.*

I stupidly had half a pint of bitter before my finals. Why, oh why, oh why? Look at me now, assistant head of Rubrics at the Oxford and Cambridge Examinations Board.

Still, can't sit here jawing all day.

- *Answer* ONE *question from* SECTION **A**. TWO *questions from* SECTION **B** *and three from* SECTION . . . *no, no, that's not right.* TWO *questions from* SECTION **A**, *surely? No, I was right the first time.* ONE *question from* SECTION **A**.

- *If you are answering questions from* SECTION **D** *do* **not** *answer questions from* SECTION **B**. *Do* **not** *answer questions from* SECTION **G** *and do* **not** *look vacantly around the room. There's bound to be some slip of a* GIRL *sitting just in front of you wearing a* **thin jersey** *with her* BRA STRAP *showing palely through her* TOO-THIN *blouse. A boy of your age thinks of* SEX *on average once every* TEN *seconds. That is one thousand and eighty times during the next* THREE *hours. Doesn't give you much time to apply yourself to whether* HAMLET *was mad or not. Still.*

- *Candidates who are taking this paper as part of the* HOME ECONOMICS EXAMINATION *should answer questions* FOUR *and* THREE *in* SECTION **A**. *Why, oh why is it always sunny when the exams are on? Eh? Everybody else out there lazing around and you're stuck in here with that lump on your middle finger getting bigger by the minute.*

- *Do* **not** *leave* EARLY. *That's very annoying.*

- *Do* **not** *talk about the exam endlessly over lunch.*

- *If you require more paper raise your arm and pray the invigilator isn't looking out of the window, reading his* ROBERT LUDLUM *or looking at the girl in the* **see-through blouse**.

- *Do* **not** *make a noise, or he'll think you're trying to* CHEAT.

- *Do indicate clearly whether you want more paper, or to go to the lavatory. You will regret having to* PISS *into a cone of ruled paper. It's equally annoying to the marker to have to read '*BRONCO' *every second word.*

- *Do* **not** *moan, sniff, dribble or cry.*

- *Do* **not** *sob hysterically and run screaming from the room, especially if you are the invigilator.*

- *Remember exams are terrible, but not as bad as continuous assessment.*

SECTION A

1. *"Hamlet is the mild cigar from Benson and Hedges."* Discuss in relation to the character of the second grave-digger.

RULES FOR PLAYING

C L U E L E S S

The eighteen cards are shuffled. Three are removed and placed in
• THE MYSTERY ENVELOPE •
and the rest are dealt among the players face down.

THERE ARE SIX CHARACTERS

MISS BLUE • MS. REDBRIGADE • MR. WHITE

Porno queen and police briber   Urban terrorist   The cocaine dealer

MR. PEA-COCK • MR. BLACK • REV. PINK-OBOE

The psychopath with a small-penis obsession   14-year-old West Indian victim of society   The gay vicar of Wandsworth

SIX MURDER WEAPONS

THE CRICKET BALL ON THE END OF A WIRE
THE NYLON STOCKING FILLED WITH £1 COINS
THE BAZOOKA AND CLUSTER BOMB
THE HEROIN OVERDOSE • THE F1-11 JET
THE MOTORWAY FLYOVER PILLAR

SIX SCENES FOR THE MURDER

THE INDOOR KARZEY
THE OUTDOOR KARZEY
THE ADVENTURE PLAYGROUND
THE DISUSED RAILWAY TUNNEL
OUTSIDE MACDONALD'S
THE SUPPLEMENTARY BENEFITS OFFICE

THE OBJECT OF THE GAME

Find out who did the murder, where they did it and how.
This is done in the following ways:

LOOKING AT THE THREE CARDS BEFORE THEY
GO INTO THE MYSTERY ENVELOPE
BRIBING SOMEONE WHO KNOWS
BEATING UP SOMEONE WHO KNOWS

There are two dice. These may be thrown when you're bored with
CLUELESS; which is usually after five minutes. There has just been
released a major feature film based on the boardgame CLUELESS.
We strongly recommend "Jewel of the Nile" instead.

RAZOR EDDIE'S
guide to eating out

Chinese Style

Which cuisine?

There are many different styles of Oriental cuisine – the best-known in this
country being Pekin-style or Cantonese-style. To avoid confusion, the best
thing to do is to lump them together under the general heading of 'Chinky'.
(Either: EAT HEEL or TEKAWAY.)

When seated in the restaurant, the first and foremost thing to do is to hold
up the fork and spoon and address the waiter, thus: 'Oi! Mao Tse-tung!
Give us some chopsticks. I wish to show off to my friends.'

Using chopsticks

The first thing to remember is that the two chopsticks are quite different.
One is the top one and one is the bottom one. Sometimes they are difficult to
tell apart, being the same size and shape. The top one is the one with the
禾 character on it. (The ancient Chinese symbol for the fire-dragon being
chased by the maidens of Schuzen who have just turned into doves with
golden feathers.) The bottom one has the 禾 character on it. (The ancient
Chinese symbol for the man who repairs automatic Durex dispensing
machines.)

FIRST Hold the bottom one thus

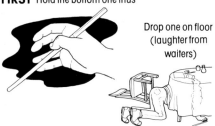

Drop one on floor (laughter from waiters)

SECOND This is the right way

Here are a few of the wrong ways:

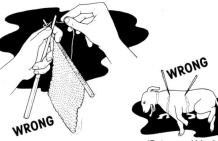

WRONG

WRONG

WRONG
(But a good idea)

WRONG
(Unless you're trying to leave without paying)

WRONG
(Unless they're playing piped Mantovani)

Finally – just before the food arrives – always remember to call the waiter,
saying: 'Oi! Hoo Flung-dung! Give us me fork and spoon back!'

EUROPEAN ELECTION COMMUNICATION

Why should I be your representative in the European Parliament?
Well, why not?
says front-running Euro-candidate
MELVYN KENNETH SMITH

" Let's face it, the average man in the street, ordinary Joe Public, the proverbial man on the Clapham tramcar knows very little about the European Parliament. (Or to give it its full title: *European assembly thing in Brussels or Geneva or Strasbourg or somewhere, you know, isn't Barbara Castle in it?*) **CAN REPRESENT THAT MAN.** I identify with him. I don't know anything about the European Commission either. I think the whole Common Market business wastes millions of pounds on French farmers, giving butter to the Russians, that sort of thing, but I don't suppose there's much anybody can do about it now. So let me represent **YOUR EUROPEAN CONSTITUENCY.**

■ I travel well. No air sickness on all of those jolly cross-channel flights.
■ I eat well. I undertake to make the most of the generous expenses on the Euro-gravy train. Remember I will be scoffing for Britain. Why let the fat krauts get their noses in the trough?
■ I am semi bi-lingual.
■ I am prepared to go to the ends of the Earth to get things done (or at least discussed) for Britain, Europe and the world (if I am paid to do it).
■ I am prepared to sleep through a debate conducted in any of the major European languages.
Quite frankly who cares who goes to Europe? What is

the name of your current European representative? What is the name of your European constituency? Have you heard of your representative making a speech or anything? There you are then . . .
Stop trying to put Europe on the map and start putting me into the cushiest job going. "

FOR A GREAT DEAL (FOR HIM) VOTE SMITH ☒

The Observer's Book Of Turds

№ 2 Dog Turds

The Common Pavement Ornamenter

● *Familiar resident in cities, towns and beauty-spots in all parts of the mainland Britain. Colour varies from a rich mahogany to mustard yellow. Length: 3-6 in (some male specimens even larger). Also called Turnstomach from the feelings of nausea it induces by turning up on children's fingers, pram wheels, footballers' knees etc.*

The Lesser Spotted Squelch

● *The joker of the turd world, this cheeky character has low-lying habits which make it difficult for the non-turd-watcher to spot. It is usually detected when your foot lands on it with a distinctive squelch – which gives it its name. Reproduces asexually, being rapidly spread by humans wiping their feet along pavements, kerbs and other people's carpets.*

The Old White Crumbly

● *Slow-maturing turd which may survive for many years in undisturbed locations such as roadside verges, tower-block walkways, BR station platforms etc. Typically, it has the texture and taste of Parmesan cheese. (Well. Try it yourself if you don't believe us.)*

The Great Dribbler

● *Not a true turd but a puddle of evil-smelling liquid associated with the sort of stray dogs which feed out of dustbins and poodles that shiver a lot. Frequently attracted to shopping-centres, it is common all over Europe but thought to be extinct in Switzerland.*

Band Wagon

'We'll Never Work Again'

(Soulfully)
Showbusiness is a wonderful world,
When you're young and rich and famous,
But when the work is hard to come by,
And the hits are few and far between,
(You wait for death and disaster)
And pretend you're still a star.

(Omnes)
So sing a charity song,
With headphones on,
And remind the paying public
Who you are.

We are clapped out,
We are the has-beens,
We're cashing in on a good idea
Band Aid once had,
We're cashing in on a good idea
Band Aid once had.

We've made this video
To let the people know,
We're available for cabaret bookings,
Throughout the land.

(Solo)
I'm a DJ
I wear a toupee.

(Solo)
I am the sister of someone's cousin
who's in a band,
You've forgotten I exist,
And I'm completely pissed
But now you know what a marvellous
girl I really am.

(Omnes)
We are clapped out,
We are the has-beens,

We're doing this for charity,
'Cos we need publicity,
And charity begins at home,
When your act's this bad.

Orchestra sequence into:
Sign on,
Sign on,
If this song ain't a hit,
'Cos we'll never work again.
Yeah.
We'll never work again.

Fade, with sobbing and moaning.

Words and music by Marsden-Krezmer
This is a charity record in aid of the victims
of Pamela Stephenson's one-woman show

The Band Wagon: Gerry Marsden; the only one from Genesis not to have a solo career; Mike Merkin, Radio Mercia DJ; Colin Shapiro (Helen Shapiro's son); Jimmy Mulville (the ginger one from *Who Dares Wins*. You know him. He's quite famous, really. At least, his girl-friend thinks so); Mike Winters, Bernie Winters; Gummo Winters; Zeppo Winters; Johnny Winters; Freddy Garrety; Miss Milk Marketing Board 1976 (The Dairy Queen); the man who appeared on the *Generation Game* and sang 'Mule train' while banging himself on the head with a tin tray; Judy Carne; Trevor Little, TV's comedy balloonist; Raymond Baxter; Gordon (from Peter and Gordon); Mike (Wombles) Batt; Norman (Dreadful) Vaughan; the latest smug young wanker on *That's Life*; Peter Gordeno; Beaky (from Dave Dee, Dozy, Beaky, Mick and Titch); Long John Baldry; Short John Baldry; Medium-Sized John Baldry and countless others too feeble to mention.
All these artistes have given their services absolutely free, some of them foregoing their usual £5 cabaret fee.

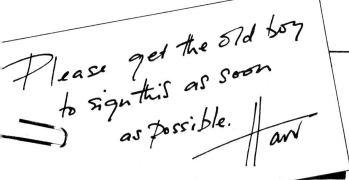

Please get the old boy to sign this as soon as possible. Harv

AN AGREEMENT made the   day   of   between the HARVEY GOLDSTEIN COMPANY LIMITED (hereinafter called 'the Promoter' which expression shall be deemed to include its successors in title licensees and assigns) of the one part and

HIS HOLINESS POPE JOHN PAUL II GOD'S VICAR ON EARTH

hereinafter called 'the Artiste' (which expression shall be deemed to include his successors in title) of the other part

WHEREBY IT IS AGREED AS FOLLOWS:

1   The Artiste will
celebrate one (1) full Tridentine Mass at each of the following locations on the dates specified:

Westminster Cathedral   (3 May)
Liverpool Cathedral (R.C.)   (6 May)
Q.P.R. Football Stadium, Loftus Rd, W12   (8 May) *
Mecca Bingo, Wolverhampton   (10 May)
Upstairs Room, King's Head, Upper Street, N1 (12, 13, 14 May)

*If wet in BBC TV Theatre, Shepherd's Bush Green (vacate in time for Wogan)

2   Prior to each of the events in (1) above the Artiste will
drive for a minimum distance of 1½ miles (3km) along roads open to the public in a vehicle to be provided by the Promoter which for all purposes will be known as THE POPEMOBILE. Whilst being so driven the Artiste will wave to the crowds and bless them in any of the following languages: English, Latin, Polish, Italian, Urdu (Wolverhampton only).

3   On arrival at Heathrow Airport   the Artiste will   kiss the tarmac (ACT AS SEEN) in full view of the cameras of both BBC and ITN.

4   In all publicity   the Artiste's name will appear immediately above and in letters similar in size or larger than God's and immediately below Harvey Goldstein's.

5   Each celebration of Mass will be required to last for a minimum of one (1) hour. (NO ENCORES.)

6   On signature of this agreement the promoter will pay to the credit of
POPETOURS LTD, Unit 15, Vatican City, nr Rome, Italy,
£150,000 (one hundred and fifty thousand pounds, no pence)
as an advance against a 30 per cent share of the total take from all entrance fees, collections, licences and other financial arrangements made by the Promoter in connection with   the Artiste's tours of England.

7   This agreement is subject to the Schedule which is on the reverse and forms part of this agreement.

8   In any dispute as to the construction of the terms of this Agreement and the Schedule thereto the Artiste's decision will be infallible.

Signed on behalf of Harvey Goldstein Ltd ....

Signed on behalf of   the Pope   ....

SCHEDULE

(i)   At each venue the Artiste will be provided with a dressing room with ensuite bathroom (<u>not shower</u>).

(ii)   Backstage passes (access all areas) will be issued to the following:
The Pope's immediate entourage of <u>UP TO NINE</u> Cardinals and <u>TEN</u> general acolytes
PLUS
Fr. Franco Sinatro (Voice coach)
Fr. Edwardo Giovene (Sound and P.A.)
Brother Anthony of Genoa (Lighting & Popemobile maintenance)
Fr. Tardeli, or substitute (Pedicurist)
Fr. Stephano di Tagliatelli Verde (Manicurist)
Cardinal Basil Hume (Westminster Cathedral only)
Sister Kim il Santoya and Sister Kim il Suk (Masseuses)
Henry Schwarzkoff and Henry Niegart (Gag writers)

(iii)   No backstage pass will be issued to Mr Norman St John Stevas (or anyone looking remotely like him).

(iv)   For use in the performances the promoter will provide 4 cwt. of Fortnum & Mason's Tasty Papal Wafers ('Melt in the mouth, not in the priest's hand') and <u>900</u> litres of Valpolicella Full-Bodied Red Wine.

(v)   Facilities for make-up to be approved by the Pope's make-up consultant Cardinal Fifi Salvatorini.

(vi)   <u>AT EVERY PERFORMANCE</u> there will be provided for the Artiste:
1 case of Polish vodka
2 bottles of Holy Water (non-carbonated)
1 barrel of oysters
1 box After Eight mints
10 rounds smoked salmon sandwiches
1 lb. caviare
1½ pints of cabbage soup
1 box Havana cigars (Romeo & Julietta)

(vii)   Dry cleaning facilities will be made available to the Artiste at the Promoter's expense for the following:
2 capes
1 cassock
3 vestments
4 sets silk underwear

(viii)   To avoid tasteless commercial exploitation of the Artiste's tour, no product connected with the Artiste will be put on sale to the public or licensed for sale by the promoter without prior permission from Prior G. Crazzi, POPETOURS (COMMERCIAL) LTD, Unit 15, Vatican City, nr Rome, Italy. (Those currently licensed include ACTION-PONTIFF Pope Dolls and ''CAROL SAYS DON'T DO IT'' T-shirts.)

RUN FOR YOUR MONEY

The West-End Farce

By Ray Cooney and Richard Stilgoe

SCENE. – *Interior of a West-End theatre on Shaftesbury Avenue.*

It is three o'clock in the afternoon. The theatre is in need of redecoration. The walls of the auditorium are painted a nasty reddish brown and decorated with large plaster female figures with bits broken off. The effect is similar to a Turkish brothel. There are approximately seven hundred seats covered in Dralon and improbably numbered somewhere at ground level. Fifteen of the seats are occupied. Door opening off to bars L.I.E., L.U.E. *Girl dressed in black waistcoat, long skirt and training shoes* L.C. *She is clutching a large pile of "Souvenir Programmes" retailing at seven pounds fifty. As the curtain rises, we hear: (distinctly)* OLD LADY – *asking for her hearing aid; incomprehensible Japanese dialogue in which the words* STARLIGHT EXPRESS *are audible* L.C.; *extended childish shouting.*

CURTAIN MUSIC: *"The Plagiarist" by A. L. Webber. First sixteen bars inaudible. Second sixteen bars deafening. Abrupt end in the middle of next bar. The* CURTAIN *rises unexpectedly. On the* STAGE *is a representation of a suburban middle-class living-room. It bears an uncanny resemblance to the drawing-room of the Beatons in the 1975 Leicester Haymarket production of Alan Ayckbourn's "No Pun in the Title". It is in need of some redecoration. This is* TONY's *living-room.* TONY *is an impoverished writer. His living-room measures seventy feet by fifteen, and has walls twenty feet tall. It is decorated in late-nineteen-sixties, with furniture borrowed from "The Importance of Being Earnest" (Swansea Rep). The time is the present.* THIRTY SECONDS *after the* CURTAIN MUSIC *ends, the lights go up on the* STAGE.

Enter TONY, *through upstage right door. He bangs door shut. The walls of living-room wobble. N.B. During the scene this door will open of its own accord twice and swing outward to reveal the* UNDERSTUDY *waiting for her next entrance with a copy of the script in her hands.*

TONY *is a middle-aged character actor. He once had a leading role in "Z Cars" and now is best known for advertising a leading brand of electrical do-it-yourself appliance on certain regional television stations. His face is artificially tanned – in marked contrast to his ears, hands and the forepart of his arms which stick out of his jacket, which is too small for him. His hair is dark blue. He is playing the part of* JULIAN.

He is unsteady on his feet. He crosses Down Stage Left with four paces exactly.

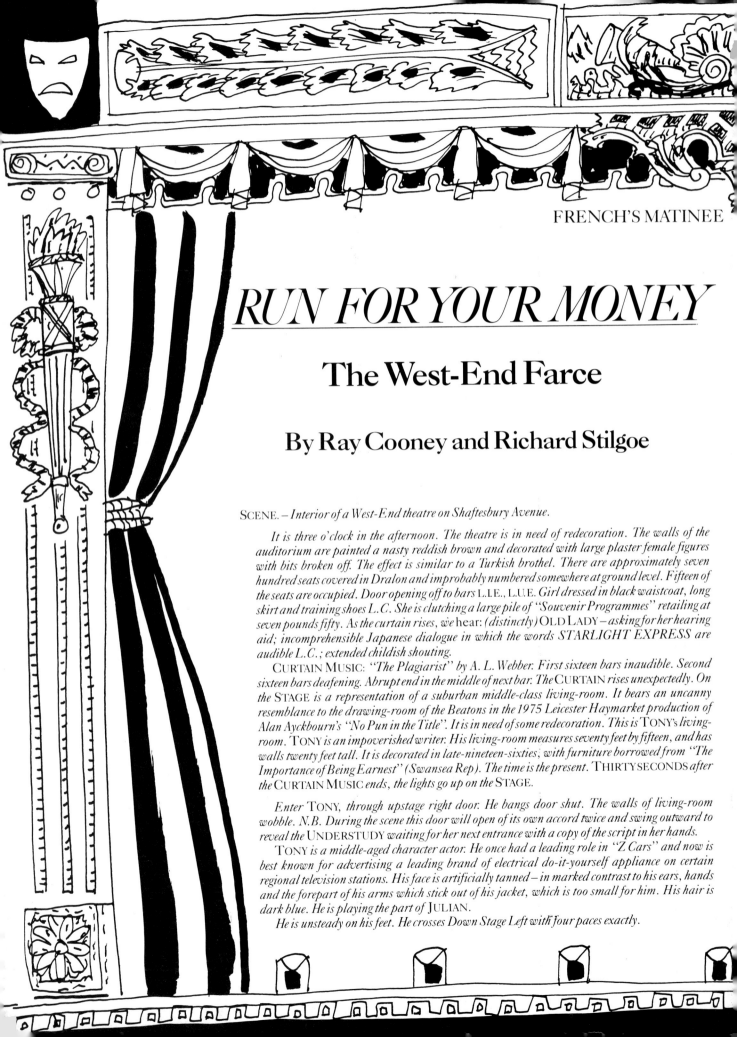

TONY (*with weary resignation of one saying a line for the 320th time*). Margot!! (*He crosses to the corner cabinet Down Stage Left, shaking his head as he goes to indicate he is acting. He pours himself a generous slug of cold tea.*)

(*From the Auditorium there is the sound of a* MAN *entering the theatre.*)

MAN (*with booming sotto voce*). I am a member of the profession, my dear. I have simply mislaid my ticket. Let me tell you I am a personal friend of the leading man. (TONY *turns and glares into the auditorium.*)

MAN. Cooooooeeeee! Tony!

TONY (*with a note of desperation*). Margot!!!

There is a slight rattle of the doorhandle Up Stage Left. After a momentary pause, it is followed by an extended rattle of the same doorhandle.

TONY'*s eyes glaze over. He crosses to the cabinet, Down Stage Left, to top up his cold tea from another bottle labelled "Sainsbury's Own Brand Malt Whisky".*

Enter MARGOT, *Down Stage Left, through a small gap between the edge of the set and the proscenium arch. She is holding the doorhandle.* MARGOT *is a very distinguished middle-aged actress with a string of successful hit situation comedies to her credit. She has a migraine. She is not in the theatre this afternoon. Her place is taken by* SANDY, *a twenty-four-year-old neurotic making her first professional appearance since leaving drama school seven years ago.* SANDY *crosses Stage Left. She holds on to the furniture. She stops directly upstage of* JULIAN *and adjusts a grey wig which has begun to slip down over her eyes.*

SANDY (*quiveringly*). Hello, Jeremy.

TONY (*with an expression that allows the audience to see that his dentures gleam oddly in stage lighting*). Julian!!

MAN IN AUDITORIUM (*loudly*). Haw! Haw! Haw!

There is a pause. TONY *places his hands firmly on Margot's shoulders and positions her next to a side-table.*

SANDY (*blinking*). Julian. Oh, god. Sorry. (*She reaches out with her left hand and grips the side-table which teeters and sends a table lamp crashing to the floor. There is a very long pause, during which* SANDY *looks like a horse frightened by thunder.* TONY *looks like a middle aged character actor waiting for a cue.*)

(*From the Auditorium comes the high-pitched whine of a hearing-aid on the blink.*)

TONY *crosses to the sideboard, Up Stage Right. He is staring into the wings intensely. He pauses and picks up the telephone. The telephone rings.*)

TONY. Ah – hello. Yes… Fine… OK… We'll expect you at seven. Bye. (*This last speech is rendered inaudible because the telephone continues to ring throughout.*

TONY. That was the Hendersons. They're coming over with their daughter Jane, their uncle, Colonel Bumshaw, and the very attractive German au pair. I must just iron my trousers. (*He starts to remove his trousers.*)

(*From the Auditorium there is the sound of seven Japanese tourists exiting with feeling.*)

K HART. 86

1986
A RIGHT ROYAL YEAR TO REMEMBER

Not since 1953 when the Queen was crowned and climbed Everest with Sherpa Tennison has there been a royal year like it! **Incredibly** *all these historic royal events happened in this* **one** *amazing year…*

☆ **THE QUEEN'S 60th BIRTHDAY** ☆

☆ ☆ **THE MARRIAGE OF** ☆
PRINCE ANDREW AND LADY FERGIE ☆

THE DEATH OF THE DUCHESS OF WINDSOR

THE 5th WEDDING ANNIVERSARY OF BOTH PRINCE CHARLES *AND* LADY DI

★ *ALL IN ONE YEAR!* ★

Whatever happened to Peters & Lee?

The Spanish Civil War

ANTHOLOGISED

SPAIN IN 1937

Republican

PORTUGAL

Intersun

Cosmos

Nationalist

Thompsons

"A Sea of Mud and Gazpacho"
An Old Pouf Remembers.

AUBREY SIMPSON LEWIS was a young poet in the thirties. He went to Spain on 1 May 1938 to see for himself the carnage, the blood, the sweat and the heat of battle. He came back on 2 May.

"To me, Spain possessed a terrifying beauty. Like a frozen Chicken. It was something to do with all that death. Death was everywhere you went, and let's face it, Death is an awfully good subject for poetry. It rhymes with Breath, for example, and Wreath. (Or does it? No, not really, I suppose. Still, it's better than Oxford. That hardly rhymes with anything. Or College! That only rhymes with Porridge.)"

SIMPSON LEWIS SHORTLY BEFORE HE ACCIDENTALLY SHOT HIMSELF IN THE HEAD.

GENERAL FRANCO SHAKES HANDS WITH THE INVISIBLE MAN ON THE STEPS OF LA CORTE.

Lines on the fall of Madrid.

So,
We're off to Sunny
Spain, Oh!
Viva
Espagna.
Yes,
We're off to Sunny
Spain, Oh!
Viva
Espagna.
Ohhhh.
We're off to Sunny
Spain, Oh!
Viva
Espagna.
Espagna por favor.
Oi!

FABER & FABER, 1939.

BUCK MEIHEIMER was an American who went to Spain as a journalist, and came back a man. He went on to write his novel about the war, "FLESH AND FLOWERS", which won a Nobel Prize for Botany:

"There were lots of different nationalities about down there. It was kinda weird, see. There were English and French, and short dark hairy people that I took to be Scandinavians. There were Hungarians and Slovaks and Welsh. But we were all together. You could feel it. We were all united in one common cause. Every one of us hated the Belgians."
"WHO'S THAT BELL TOLLING FOR?" GARLIC PRESS, 1948.

GENERALISSIMO GONZALEZ PEDRONE fought for the Nationalists. He is now retired, apart from trips to Madrid for his weekly attempted coup.
"And then there came the Golden Times. By Jove, but we pulled some fingernails. Nowadays you can't even attach an electrode to somebody's goolies without getting Amnesty bloody International on the blower."
"REACH FOR THE THUMBSCREWS", PARADOR, 1979.

IRISH SUBMARINE SURFACES IN THE FOOTHILLS OF THE SIERRA DE GUADARRAMA.

Dirge

Barcelona is bleeding.
Barcelona is bleeding.
Barcelona is bleeding
Hot.
But it's better than an Oxford college,
Which is grey and dull,
And rather like porridge . . .
EXTRACT FROM "COLLECTED SHORTER POEMS",
NEW LEFT BOOK CLUB AND INSURANCE BROKERS, 1942.

DENNIS NORDEN was not at the Spanish Civil War, he knows nothing about it, but he does have an opinion on anything that happened over twenty years ago:

"I remember when Vesta Tilley first met Margie Scrogget at the Leicester Alhambra, now sadly . . ."

THE REBELS COME TO A STANDSTILL WHEN ALL THEIR TANKS ARE WHEEL-CLAMPED BY THE MADRID POLICE.

LORD BUSBY was a minister in the last pre-war government, Home Secretary for much of the war and an historian and journalist. He is now best remembered for making fatuous comments in a deep booming voice on "Any Questions".

"Churchill warned them over and over again, but they did not, or rather would not, listen. I think it was because he could not pronounce his esses properly. "Spain", "Spanish", and so on. Whenever he said words like that he would spray you with saliva, and people just turned their heads away."
"THE HISTORY OF EUROPE. MY OWN STORY",
PLAYBOY BOOKS, 1976.

"The Nationalists were terrifying; the Black Death Brigade frightened us; the Bone Crusher Division were horrifying; the Use-Your-Testicles-for-Doorstops Corps really gave us the shits; but for sheer bloody-minded horror you couldn't beat the Regiment of Spanish Air-Traffic Controllers".
A. SIMPSON LEWIS, "HOMAGE TO CATALONIA",
WAR PICTURE LIBRARY, 1967.

THE CAST OF THE 1934 FOOTLIGHTS REVUE CHEERIO BARCELONA "MAN" THE ARTILLERY. (L TO R JACK HULBERT, RICHARD MURDOCH, JONATHON MILLER, JOHN CLEESE AND RICHARD STILGOE.)

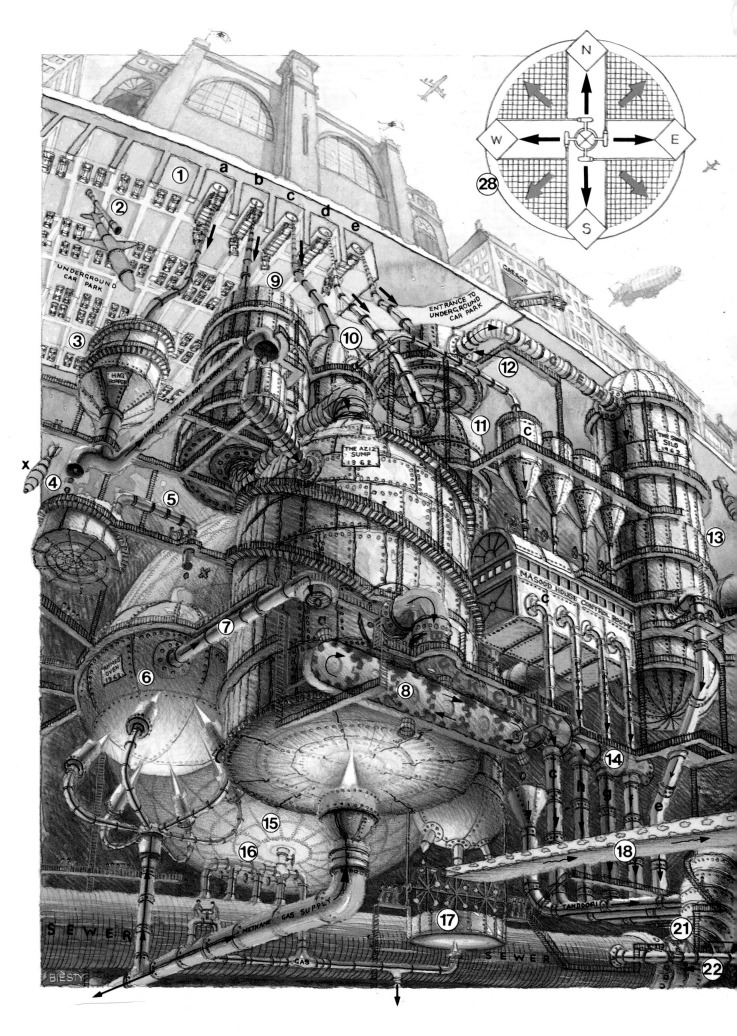

* 20,000 Indian nosheries in Inner London
* Over 100,000 tons of curry swallowed every night
* Have you ever wondered how it is possible for your order to be dealt with so quickly?
   Well, now we can reveal…

THE LONDON CURRY CONNECTION
— How the metropolitan demand for curry is met —

* Yes. Beneath the streets of London is an incredible labyrinth of tunnels and pipes that is comparable with the sewage network in more ways than one.
* All Indian restaurants are linked to the same gigantic kitchen situated directly beneath King's Cross station. And nightly, beneath London's streets, the Madras flows…

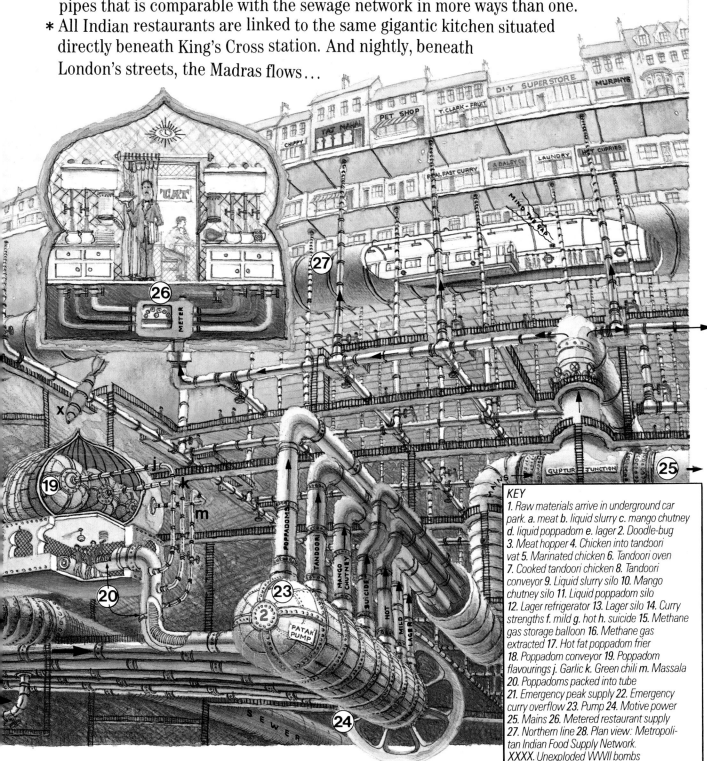

KEY
1. Raw materials arrive in underground car park. a. meat b. liquid slurry c. mango chutney d. liquid poppadom e. lager 2. Doodle-bug 3. Meat hopper 4. Chicken into tandoori vat 5. Marinated chicken 6. Tandoori oven 7. Cooked tandoori chicken 8. Tandoori conveyor 9. Liquid slurry silo 10. Mango chutney silo 11. Liquid poppadom silo 12. Lager refrigerator 13. Lager silo 14. Curry strengths f. mild g. hot h. suicide 15. Methane gas storage balloon 16. Methane gas extracted 17. Hot fat poppadom frier 18. Poppadom conveyor 19. Poppadom flavourings j. Garlic k. Green chili m. Massala 20. Poppadoms packed into tube 21. Emergency peak supply 22. Emergency curry overflow 23. Pump 24. Motive power 25. Mains 26. Metered restaurant supply 27. Northern line 28. Plan view: Metropolitan Indian Food Supply Network. XXXX. Unexploded WWII bombs

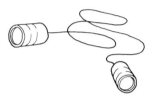

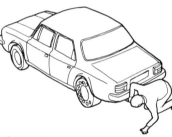

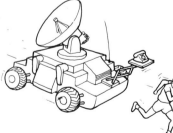

MAMMON
INTERNATIONAL plc

Are just a bunch of dishonest shysters out to make a quick buck*

Which is why the directors of UNITED INDUSTRIES plc **UNANIMOUSLY** recommend shareholders to accept their offer.

*stock exchange figures

OVER71

JUNE 1987 75p

DRUGS: A NATIONWIDE PROBLEM
Is your doctor giving you enough?

50 – A DIFFICULT AGE
Coping with your children's menopause

WHICH WALKING FRAME?
We test hobble the new Alumino Turbo with the go-fast handles

CHANGING YOUR WILL TO IRRITATE YOUR FAMILY

OWNING UP TO 80
Kenneth Williams comes out of the closet

BRRR!! IT'S NIPPY
Beat hypothermia with our new sex techniques

ARE YOU GAGA?

Try our 10 minute test and win tickets to *3-2-1*

PLUS *Do older men make good lovers? Our Centenarians' Sex Survey. Shirley Conran reports back. Keep young and beautiful. Aerobics with Malcolm Muggeridge.*

AND *all our regular whinges, moans and complaints.*

MEN'S FASHION SUPPLEMENT *Smelly trousers are back again for autumn. Soup stain of the month. Demob suits—have they finally had it?*

T'Committee

Brian Clough (Chief Whippet).

Barbara Castle (Head of T'Ladies Committee).

Russell Harty (Assistant Head of T'Ladies Committee)

MUCK ~ BRASS

THE ASSOCIATION OF
PROFESSIONAL NORTHERNERS

Incorporating
The Union Of Allied Mankdrobblers & Buntweavers

— T'Agenda —

REPORT ON
T' ANNUAL GENERAL MEETING, DINNER and AWARDS CEREMONY
Held in the upstairs room of T'Association's favourite public house,
"The Long Pockets and Short Arms".

GUESTS ARRIVE AND GRUMBLE 'BOUT T'BUS FARES
COCKTAILS
COMPLAINTS 'BOUT SHORT MEASURES
DINNER
COMPLAINTS 'BOUT EFFECTS OF RICH FOOD ON T'COLOSTOMY BAGS
SPEECHES
DESPONDENT GROUSIN' 'BOUT LENGTH O' T'SPEECHES
AWARDS
ARGUMENT CUM BRAWL 'BOUT WHO'S PAYING FER T'EVENING

During t'arrival of guests and dinner, t'band of t'Professional Northern Dance Orchestra
and t'Brighouse and Rastrick Colliery Brass Ensemble played selections from t'Hovis
advert. It were reet beltin'.

— T'Menu —

An a'p'eth of Wazzock Soup
served in a brass kecklin' bowl

Bloater Butties, served with "Wilfred" Pickles
or
Boil in the Bag Meat & Gravy

Dollops o' Jam Puddin'

All served wi' a bottle o' some fancy French plonk that
tastes like a wet Tuesday in Ormskirk and we'd be better off
drinkin' us own detritus and a damn sight cheaper an' all

Processing
T'Wazzock
From oop North
to Camden Town

T'Wazzock leaves Barnsley.

Extras from T'Hovis advertisement ga[...]
to cheer T'Wazzock through Grantha[...]

Arthur Scargill (in full ceremonial dress).

T'Awards Ceremony

The ringin' of an owd tram bell announced serious business of t'speeches. Chief borer 'i'self, **Colin "fat git wi' a perm" Welland** addressed assembled in a thick guttural accent and spake of 'is childhood in a thick gutter in Wigan and of 'is adulthood in Kensington and Chelsea. The audience remained dour throughout the entire speech and showed their appreciation at t'end by knockin' out their pipes on their steel-capped boots.

Then cam' t'award ceremony. An 'ush descended over t'assembled bores, pedants and tight-wads. Chairlad 'i'self, **Michael "pickled walnut mush" Parkinson** rose to his wallet, doffed his cap to t'gaffer **Freddie Truman** and announced winners of **1986 Professional Northerner Awards.**

For long service to t'society, the **Golden Flogged Dead Horse** went to **Bill Tidy** for his relentless persistence in trying to make fish and chips funny. On the **Larry Grayson** table, **Alan Bennett, Russell Harty** and **Mike Harding** gathered their shawls around them and rattled their sherry glasses in approval.

The Silver Cobblestone for most Over-the-top and gratuitous use of a Northern Accent on Television went as usual to **Molly Sugden** who folded her arms and wobbled her boozum with delight ... as did **Alan Bennett** and **Russell Harty**.

The Golden Boycott for Outstanding Bigotry went to **Arthur Scargill** who with characteristic dry humour refused to accept the award. Ee, we all fell about.

The Association's top award, **The Gracie**, for Lifelong Northernism went to **Barbara Castle** (or possibly **Thora Hird**... it were difficult to see with only a 60-watt lightbulb illuminating a 2000-seat auditorium). There was a reverent silence (even the knitting at the **Larry Grayson** table stopped) as **Barbara Castle** or **Thora Hird** hobbled, creaking as she went, to the podium where previous winner of the award **Harold 'a week's a long time on Neptune' Wilson** waited to present the award, issuing forth thick clouds of malodorous smog from his pipe filled with Bleasdale's Blackstuff.

There were tumultuous clapping. **Roy Hattersley** took a sip of t'pint 'es hired out for t'full hour and from the Grayson table came the joyous banging of mascara brushes.

Then came the crescendo of the evening. Everybody was upstanding as Penrith's favourite son **Melvyn Bragg** stepped to t'front o't'room. Melvyn had flown in by helicopter especially from 'is home in Virginia Water to lead the assembly in the Association's song.

With his familiar flat cap and his flat nose, 'is lined orange face wrinkled with pleasure as he sang the first verse of the song to t'tune of *"When the likely lads come in on a kind of loving on Sunday mornin' covered in blackstuff, pet".*

T'Song

By the jobble of me grandad's pollock,
 Wi' a knackle o' me stoddy bog's bilge,
I'd a' soon tap a shuntgrommet jollock
 Than belper in a matlock's wilge.

CHORUS:
Ear all see all say nout!
Eat all drink all pay nout!
And if ever thou does owt fer nowt ...
 Do it on prime time television in a Yorkshire accent!

It were a cracking good do. There were one awkward moment when someone offered to buy a round. 'E were obviously some gate crasher. And there were one more little bit of business but nobody stepped in it. (It were that **Anthony Burgess's** whippet, I'll be bound.)

Thora Hird (Euro MP).

Larry Grayson pulls his own.

Julie Walters orders another Mackeson from the podium.

Our David, this year's winner of the Big Girl's Blouse Award, with his acceptance speech notes.

"Wazzock is mislaid in T'Watford Gap service station.

Roy Hattersley tastes t'freshly cooked Wazzock

STRANGER THAN FICTION

PROFESSOR JACOB Z PAPPASPOOK INVESTIGATES

THE PECULIAR!!

THEY CAME BY NIGHT!!!

THE CREATURE FROM THE LOCH!!

Unidentified Flying Objects

WHEN TO SEE THEM :- WHEN YOU'RE ALONE.... WHEN YOU'RE PISSED... ON GUY FAWKES NIGHT.

WHERE TO SEE THEM :- IN THE SKY.... OUT OF THE CORNER OF YOUR EYE.... NEAR AMERICAN AIR-FORCE BASES......

WHAT TO LOOK FOR :- "THE FLYING SAUCER" OR HUB-CAP-SHAPED OBJECT. THE COMMONEST SIGHTING. USUALLY ACCOMPANIED BY A HIGH-PITCHED WHIRRING SOUND. T.V. AERIAL OPTIONAL.
COLOUR: WHITE // SILVER // WHITISH // GREYISH // SILVERY // WHITISH-GREY // GREYISH-WHITE // SILVERY-WHITE // FLYING-SAUCER-COLOURED //.

"THE CIGAR-SHAPED OBJECT" USUALLY AN OBJECT WITH A CIGAR-LIKE RESEMBLANCE. **COLOUR:** WHITISH-GREY // SILVERY // GREYISH-WHITE // HAVANA-BROWN ///.

"THE AEROPLANE-SHAPED OBJECT" OFTEN SIGHTED NEAR AIRPORTS. NO T.V. AERIALS, THOUGH OFTEN ACCOMPANIED BY AN UNEARTHLY SOUND LIKE A VACUUM CLEANER GOING IN REVERSE. OBJECT OFTEN HAS STRANGE NONSENSICAL ALIEN MARKINGS — E.G. QUANTAS, VARIG, BIWA, JAL (AND MOST BAFFLINGLY LUFTHANSA.)

"THE CAR-HEADLIGHTS-SHAPED OBJECT" EXCLUSIVELY SEEN AT NIGHT, QUITE LOW ON THE HORIZON ALMOST ALWAYS IN PAIRS.

SIGHTING TIPS: ALWAYS HAVE YOUR CAMERA HANDY (FILM IN IT IF POSSIBLE); MAKE SURE IT'S WELL OUT OF FOCUS AND TRY AND EXPOSE THE FILM WHEN UNLOADING.

NEW SIGHTING HAS **NESSIE** RETURNED?

LOCAL FISHERMAN **ANGUS MacCLUNIE** CLAIMS TO HAVE SIGHTED **NESSIE**, SCOTLAND'S OLDEST AND MOST MYSTERIOUS INHABITANT. "I WAS IN MY BOAT ON THE LOCH", SAYS SHARPED EYED MONSTER-SPOTTER MacCLUNIE, "WHEN ALL OF A SUDDEN I SAW A BLACK OBJECT BREAK THE SURFACE OF THE WATER."

SHIT-SCARED!!

WAS ANGUS ABSOLUTELY SHIT-SCARED? "NO I WASN'T. IT WAS AN OLD CAR-TYRE."

OR WAS IT?

"BUT THEN I REMEMBERED TALES OF HOW THE MONSTER COULD TAKE ON THE FORM OF OTHER OBJECTS SO YOU WOULDN'T KNOW IT <u>WAS</u> THE MONSTER. I REMEMBERED STRANGE FABLES ABOUT HOW THE SCOTTISH TOURIST BOARD GAVE <u>CASH HANDOUTS</u> FOR PICTURES OF TYRES FLOATING IN **LOCH NESS**. SO I HEADED ASHORE TO GET MY CAMERA."

WHAT THE FISHERMAN SAW

AN ARTIST'S IMPRESSION

wspaper ... page. **2.** Sta...
mast-head, as in stationed at the
mast-head'. **3.** *attrib,* as in *m.light,* etc. 1822.
Masturbate (Mæ·starbeıt). v. 1857, n [*masturbat-,* pa,
ppl. stem of L. *mastur-bare,* of unkn. origin.] *intr.* and
refl. To practise self-abuse. So **Masturbation** 1766. **1.**
Bodily self-pollution. **2.** *(fig. 1746 allus.)* Physical
self-debasement and annihilation of all moral values.
3. *(Theol. and schol. L. 1862 f. * za)* Ethically unsound
and quite intolerable habit practised by boys. **4.** *(rhet.
1600 + Rom.Antiq. incl. n. dial. & w. midl.)* Loathsome
map-like stains on sheets which give matron extra
work and for which boys are sent on long lonely runs
in the bleak greyness of the Scottish moors. **5.** *(var.
superl. 1520.)* The fires of Hell itself – may the Lord
have mercy on your soul for even reading this
definition. **6.** Heinous transgression which we, the
compilers of this up-to-date, finger-on-the-pulse-of-
current-English-usage reference book, have never
committed, God strike us down if we tell a lie. **7.** The
others may have done, but I certainly haven't, my
hand's never been near that region in my life –
please, God, you must believe me; I don't even touch
that when I go to wee-wees *(please forgive me for
saying 'wee-wees' – I could have said 'urinate' or 'pee' but
they're equally bad – oh God, what have I said? Help me.)*
8. *(etym. 1834 correl. + fig. Epil.Aram. c.1420 attrib. and
Comb. A.V. bef. 1870)* I don't want to go to Hell, Lord.
Sometimes I lie awake in bed at night just thinking
about it... and then I start thinking about IT – you
know – what we're talking about here... and then I
can't help it... it just happens... oh sweet Jesus, I'll
never do it again... I promise... **never**...**NEVER**
Matador (Mae.tâdôr). In senses 2 and 3 usu.
-ore. 1774. [Sp. *matadoree,* f. *matarr* render
dead, f. *-tadore deceased* L. *matado...*
definition is n...

★ *Is your double-act a little bit single at the moment? Have your punchlines got no feedlines?*

★ *Do you need a fat ugly clown to make you seem like the good-looking one who is really quite a good ballad singer?*

then Feedline *is for you*

Just answer these few simple questions and before long you... and your 'partner'... may have YOUR OWN SHOW! (On Saturday evenings, right after *The A Team!*)

Which of these people do you think you would find most compatible?

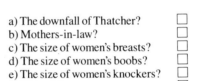

Do you consider your act...

a) Alternative? ☐
b) Old-fashioned? ☐
c) Feeble? ☐
d) Clapped-out? ☐
e) Dire? ☐
f) The pits? ☐
g) Tom O'Connor? ☐

Would you most likely do jokes about...

a) The downfall of Thatcher? ☐
b) Mothers-in-law? ☐
c) The size of women's breasts? ☐
d) The size of women's boobs? ☐
e) The size of women's knockers? ☐
f) Kids, eh? ☐
g) Farts, bums, willies, jobbies and general lavatoria? ☐
h) Irishmen and Pakis? ☐

Are you...

a) The short fat one? ☐
b) The tall one with glasses? ☐
c) The one who drops his trousers? ☐
d) The one with funny braces? ☐
e) The one who can't sing? ☐
f) The one who can't do impressions? ☐

Sex .... Age ....

Height ....

Some of Feedline's notable successes

Dear Feedline,
How can I thank you enough? Here I am, overweight, sweaty, with a modicum of talent for singing old rock songs – and a perm. All I needed for success was a skinny shortsighted little runt with an even more puerile sense of humour than me. You found him for me! Sid Little. Together we have made it to the top with most of the general public agreeing that I am the more talented of the two.
Thank you Feedline.
Yours

Eddie Large
P.S. Now that I've made it, how do I get rid of the talentless four-eyed git?

Dear Feedline,
Many thanks. You have surpassed yourself. Not only have you found me a straightman, but you've found me a straightman who is enormously fat with lank greasy hair and a huge bulbous red and purple nose! What more could I want? We get on very well – professionally and socially we never see each other. He stays out of my hair and I stay out of his bald patch. Fortunately, he is not interested in the two things that I'm interested in: sleeping and working. He is a great tax loss and I stand to make an enormous amount in residuals when he finally kicks the bucket – which shouldn't be long the way things are going.
Yours
Sir Griffith Rhys Jones
Sir Griffith Rhys Jones

Dear Feedline,
A brief note to say thank you thank you thank you thank you... Years and years in showbiz without ever really getting anywhere... constantly looking for that quirky little gimmick that would set me apart from other run-of-the-mill variety acts... and then you found me ROD HULL... and things have gone from strength to strength. Although I get a lot of stick from people saying 'How can you work with a raddled old neurotic comedian who's half foam rubber anyway?' I'm happy and I'm ever grateful to you.
Yours
EMU
Emu
P.S. Is it safe to dry-clean him?

The BIRTH alternative OF COMEDY · 1324

The "DEATH" OF COMEDY·1324 — alternative

OBITUARY

NEWTON ERIC WAYNE O.M.
"The Great Gobbo"

Newton Wayne, the world champion expectorator and gobbing millionaire, died suddenly at his Belperthwaite palace, 'Spittles', on April 14, at the age of 66.

During the 1970s and 1980s he single-handedly raised professional gobbing from a little-known minority attraction, practised in the back rooms of pubs and at illegal meetings in underground stations, to the status of a world-class sport with a television audience of millions.

Born in a spittoon in 1920, Wayne came from a long line of gobbers. His father had first practised 'throwing' in Belperthwaite in the 1930s, when the Depression hit hard, the Hovis advertisement was closed down and following a disastrous year with the whippet crop. The young Newton was weaned onto smoking bicycle inner tubes stuffed with tarmac and this, combined with the damp and smoggy air, helped develop his famed 'liquid' throat. Against his father's wishes he had early ambitions to become a boy soprano, but at the age of sixteen something stuck in his oesophagus and he soon discovered he could hit a policeman at a football match from a distance of 23 yards.

Public recognition was not long in following, and his earliest expectorations launched him on the Northern Amateur Gobbing Circuit, in a flurry of phlegm and sweat. He did not turn professional for another 7 years but supported himself as a bus driver, keeping his throat in during the day by gobbing on shoppers in the high street from his boarding platform. He never lost his love of transport, and during the years of success his collection of high-performance buses rivalled his obsession with mucus tossing.

His professional career spanned an incredible 30 years, most of it at the top. Apart from a distinguished war service in the Army Catering Corps, he was hardly ever off the 'flobber line'. He won the Guinness Golden Spittoon 21 times; the Vick's Vapour Rub Open for 5 consecutive years and the European Masters 8 times. His finest decade was the 1970s, when he was undisputed World Champion with a personal best at the 1976 World Goblet in Turkey of an astonishing 78′ 4″. He amassed a fortune on the exhibition circuit, opening clubs and closing restaurants, and brought work to his native Belperthwaite, mainly for locksmiths and burglar alarm salesmen.

He always attributed his success to hard work and practice. He was seldom without a lump in his throat and had windscreen wipers fitted to the *inside* of his turbo-driven Audi Quattrobus.

His 1983 exhibition tour of the West Indies was marred by allegations of sex and drugs parties in the company of hordes of underage gobettes, and he retired from the game two years later after a fatal accident. A referee was struck dead by one of his 70 mph 'green beauties'.

He was awarded the Order of Merit in 1979 for, amongst other things, 'raising the art of clearing the throat into a precision sport'. He leaves a wife, Muriel. They met at the Ormskirk Rainbow when she was sitting in the one-and-nines and he was up in the sixpenny gallery. She called him 'a warm feeling down the bridge of my nose'.

AIDS: NEW FACTS

A doctor writes . . .

The views of top venereologist,
Dr L. S. Brenner

[handwritten text, largely illegible]
... A.I.D.S. ...
... A.D.I.S. ...
... S.I.A.D. ...
... on TOTAL CURE FOR AIDS.

LETTERS TO
Farmer Oz

Each month, Oswald Fitzchicken,
our resident farmer and
countryman, answers your
questions about nature
and agriculture

> *Rain before noon*
> *Shower before dark*
> *Quicker than soon*
> *You'll be drenched*

Dear Oz,
    Is there really any way of predicting the weather using old rustic methods?
Yours, Theo Sprague

Dear Theo,
    Let me tell you something. On the little table in my hall, right next to the phone, I have a pair of little pine cones, which I picked from a young tree about thirty or forty years ago. Whenever I'm a bit qualmy about the weather, I go to that table and pick up the phone and I'm on to the Meteorological Society Long-range Prognosis Department (ask for Professor Schallbaum) quicker than you can say: 'I must remember to throw those bloody pine cones out!'
Oz.

Dear Oz,
    I came across this footprint in my garden last night.
    Is this a fox, or just a dog?
Yours, Bernie O'Brien

Dear Bernie,
    I'm happy to tell you it's neither. It was obviously made by a felt-tipped pen, probably containing black ink.
Oz.

Dear Oz,
    Seriously though. What animal has a footprint like that?
Yours, Bernie

Dear Bernie,
    Yes, it's definitely a fox. A microscopic, one-legged fox, by the look of it. Ha ha ha.
Oz.

Dear Oz,
    Piss off,
Yours, Bernie

> *Red sky at night —*
> *shepherd's delight!*
> *Red sky in the morning —*
> *shepherd's warning!*
> *Minced meat and mashed potatoes —*
> *shepherd's pie!*

The Horseshoe: An old country good-luck charm — but not so lucky for Tom Finch who was standing underneath when they dropped out of a cargo 'plane.

> *Starve a cold*
> *Feed a fever*
> *Give an aardvark little bits*
> *of chopped earthworms*

Dear Oz,
    When I was clearing out my great grandmother's attic I came across this statuette. Do you think it's worth anything?
Yours, June Pringle.

Dear Mrs Pringle,
    Sorry to disappoint you, it's basically just a worthless piece of rubble. But don't throw it out. Send it to me immediately . . . I may have a spare plaster arm I can stick on it, you never know. I'll send you the postage and packing for your trouble. Better luck next time.
Oz.

Dear Oz,
    Actually it's MR. Pringle. I'm called June because I happened to have been born in June. So watch it.
Yours, Mr. June Pringle

Dear Mr June Pringle
    How the bloody hell was I supposed to know? Damned silly to be named after what you were born in. I'm not called Maternity Wing.
Oz.

> *One lark for spring*
> *Two larks for summer*
> *Five hundred larks*
> *for starting your own lark zoo*

Dear Oz,
    Unfortunately I did not have my camera with me last Sunday, but I felt I had to write and tell you something amazing that I saw while walking in the Hampshire countryside. On top of a church I saw a tall, wrought-iron penis. It was mounted on a sort of turntable and was swivelling around in the wind. What was it?
Yours, Miss H. Jones

Dear Miss Jones,
    It was a weather-cock. You win this month's £5 prize for the Feedline-of-the-Month Competition,
Oz.

COUNTY LIFE

Vol. CCLXXIXIV No. 9238   **November 3, 1986**

MISS CAMILLA RING-BINDER

Miss Camilla Ring-Binder, youngest daughter of Colonel Ring-Binder, of Bollards, Whingeing Ninny, Berkshire, and Mrs Box-Carr-Willey of The Old Dairy Unit, Boring, Herts, is to be married to the Honorable Jamie Quango-Tax-Fiddle, second son of Lord and Lady Quango-Tax-Fiddle, Maxwell House, Rotisseries, Neige de Nez, Cannes.

Have patience saith the Dog.

Oh Sod it !!!!

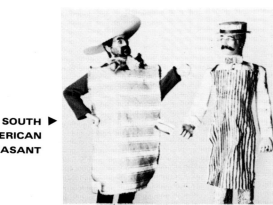

LEAGUE DIVISION IV

SCUNTHORPE	0	0	SWANSEA
TRANMERE	1	2	HALIFAX
ROCHDALE	0	1	CHESTER
TORQUAY	2	1	WREXHAM
BLACKPOOL	1	0	COLCHESTER
BORING OLD MARKET TOWN IN THE MIDDLE OF NOWHERE	1	1	OBSCURE COAL-MINING VILLAGE
DREARY SEASIDE RESORT	2	0	ANONYMOUS URBAN BARNACLE OFF THE A1
DEADLY DULL SUBURB OF SOME NORTHERN INDUSTRIAL CITY	3	0	GODFORSAKEN FISHING VILLAGE
HIDEOUS EAST MIDLANDS NONENTITY THAT DOESN'T EVEN GET A SIGNPOST AT SPAGHETTI JUNCTION	0	1	INTOLERABLY UGLY WEST COUNTRY SPRAWL THAT WASN'T HELPED BY A TOWN PLANNER HAVING A FIT ONE FRIDAY AFTERNOON
DEPRESSING HUDDLE OF ONE-UP, TWO-DOWNS AND ONE ASIAN GREENGROCER DWARFED BY THREE DERELICT REFINERIES AND AN ELECTRICITY FURNACE BELCHING GREEN SMOKE ALL DAY. TWINNED WITH A TOWN IN BELGIUM THAT DOESN'T EVEN EXIST	1	0	ALDERSHOT

THE GREAT BRITISH BARBECUE

1 **Nasty orange Dalek-shaped object** which lives in ironmongers' windows, and then in the back of a shed, emerging about once a year to ruin perfectly good food.

2 **The chef.** Note he is always a man. Long after the Stock Exchange and every other male preserve has opened its doors to women it remains the rule that outdoor cookery can only be done by men.

3 **The inevitable Australian** who drones on about 'backyard barbies' in Sydney.

4 **The irritating twat** who always tells you you should have lit the charcoal 5 hours ago if you want to get anything cooked on time.

5 **The salad bowl** emptied by guests in the hours and hours it takes to get any meat cooked.

6 **The paper plate** not quite strong enough to stop a baked potato and a burnt sausage from falling on to the grass when the person holding it tries to have a drink of wine at the same time.

7 **Chicken legs** which are burnt on the outside but frozen near the bone (only to be offered to people resistant to salmonella).

8 **Next door neighbour's dogs** which start barking as the first guest arrives and only stop 2 hours after the thunderstorm that finally washes the whole thing out.

9 **Storm clouds** which you would have expected if you hadn't been making fun of Ian McCaskill's accent during all last week's weather forecasts.

10 **Lawn** ruined by people tramping all over it, spilling drinks on it, chucking bits of cucumber, fruit, herbs, ice cubes, etc., that they have found cluttering up their drinks.

11 **Nearly empty bottle of odourless lighter fluid** whose contents you have poured on the charcoal over the past three hours and whose pungent aroma has attached itself to all the foodstuffs.

ROGET'S THESAURUS
Filofax 1-page edition

PLANTS

Nouns 1. *Plant*, vegetable, etc. etc.
2. (Varieties) legume, pea, weed, etc. etc.
3. grass, lawn, sod, and so on
4. trees, woods, forests, jungles, that sort of thing…
5. leaf, twig, other bits of plants etc.
6. seeds, flowers, other planty words

ANIMALS

Nouns 1. *Animal*, creature, synonyms for animals
2. (wild animals) hedgehog, puma, lion, etc. etc.
3. (hoofed animals) cows, other animals with hoofs [or hooves]
4. horse, gee-gee (*coll.*) pony, other words for horse
5. animal words continued

OTHER WORDS

1. words, words, words
2. more of the same

THE KING'S MALL

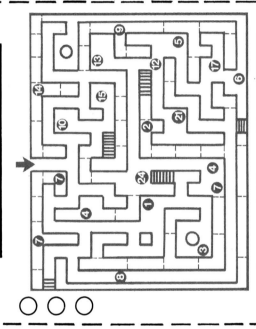

1 Large arrangements of dying rubber plants
2 Patch of liquid that never dries
3 Non-working fountains full of Coca Cola tins and chip "buckets"
4 Louts
5 Youths
6 Temporary sleeping quarters for bad-tempered meths drinkers
7 Major chain stores
8 Hot bread shop selling nothing but do'nuts
9 Vast clothing emporiums selling nothing but day-glo jackets and plastic shoes
10 Unlet shopping units with signs advertising imminent arrival of another hot bread shop
11 Exit to three remaining proper shops in the High Street
12 Vandalized electronic map with worn "YOU ARE HERE" patch
13 Broken, unbreakable, low-level orange plastic "seating" units
14 Cache of abandoned supermarket trolleys blocking exit to car park
15 Eerily deserted upper levels
16 Set of steps that go nowhere
17 Street mime artistes
18 Exit to multi-storey car park with fifteen identical unmarked levels
19 Urinal that goes up and down with sliding doors and in many other respects resembles a lift
20 30 ft by 90 ft mosaic mural depicting outstanding events in the history of the borough, defaced with spray paint
21 Remains of a green metal statue of two men and a woman with holes in their abdomens
22 Electricity showrooms
23 Bewildered old ladies
24 Escalator to upper level
25 Place where you might expect to find escalator back down to lower level except that there isn't one

1987 BEAUFORT SCALE

WIND STRENGTH		DESCRIPTION OF OBSERVED EFFECTS
0	STILL	Smoke rises vertically from Ian Botham's mouth.
1	WAFT	Empty family-size bucket of Kentucky fried chicken breast nuggets blows along pavement. Hundreds of unsold copies of *Best of Punch* flutter open exposing self-regarding, impenetrable article by Michael Bywater.
2	BREEZE	Castrol sign revolves slowly outside petrol station. Ball becomes totally uncontrollable for Arsenal's forwards.
3	WIND	Tiles fall off Richard Rogers' tower blocks. Farts are blown far enough to blame other people for them.
4	GOOD OLD BLOW	Girls on bicycles wobble as they try to steer and hold down their skirts but it's too late we've already seen their firm thighs thrusting and the tops of their tights blurring into splodgy pink bum-fat where the bicycle seat nuzzles snugly like a mischievous sniffer dog
5	CHRIST, IT'S WINDY!	Richard Rogers' tower blocks and Spanish hotels fall over. Arsenal now trailing 8-1.
6	PARDON, I CAN'T HEAR YOU FOR THE WIND	Tatty bits of doormat stuck on people's heads by blue-tack get blown off. Frankie Howerd, Paul Daniels and Bruce Forsyth stay indoors with head-scarves on.
7	TEMPEST	Impossible to read *The Times* in park. Impossible to read *The Telegraph* anywhere.
8	MACBETH	Buildings collapse. Cinemas blown about the street. Expensive hand-made Tibetan paper kite got as Christmas present stays airborne for more than ten seconds.
9	HURRICANE	Earthquakes, tidal waves, and a lock of Leslie Crowther's hair is momentarily dislodged. Arsenal's second goal ruled offside.
10	FUCK ME!	Windspeed monitor equipment blown away. Sorry.

3 **SUPER** new pages to cut out and keep!

WHOSE EYES ?

COMPETITION

Just match these famous eyes...

to their famous owner

A. *Terry Wogan* **B.** *Paul Daniels* **C.** *Liza Minelli* **D.** *Benny Hill*

THE NEW BRABHAM-LOTUS
DEATHTRAP

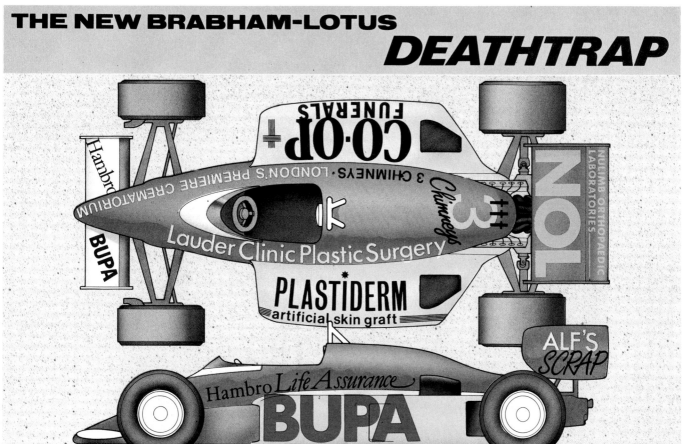

COOKING WITH
Dennis Nilsen

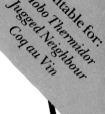

'The way to a man's heart is through his rib-cage' — ESCOFFIER

You will need

a) One 140-160 lb young, displaced homosexual (well-hung) with as little fat on him as possible
b) A strong stomach
c) A tie

Méthode (Method)

1 Joint the carcase as indicated
2 Boil thoroughly until grey

Will keep in the freezer indefinitely, in the drains for several months, under the floorboards for about a week/until the police come round (whichever is the sooner).

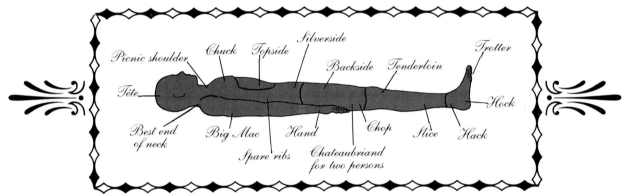

Batterie de cuisine

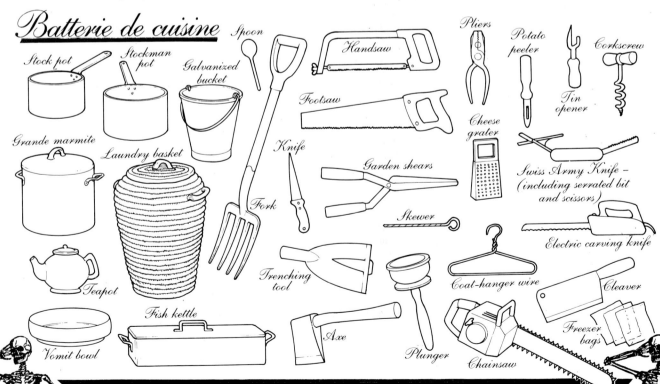

RIDLEY ROAD COMPREHENSIVE SCHOOL
RIDLEY ROAD   SOUTH RIDLEY

The Area Representative.
The National Union of Teachers

Dear Mr Simpson,

Thank you so much for your circular letter instructing all N.U.T. members to refrain from certain voluntary duties in support of the current pay claim. Now, whilst I have never taken an active part in the union's affairs I do hope that I have always been a loyal member to be counted on in a crisis. (You may incidentally rest assured that the question of my outstanding subscription will be dealt with as soon as possible.) But I am bound to say that I found some aspects of your communication rather puzzling.

For example you say we should refuse to 'cover' for an absent colleague. Well, the last time I took another teacher's class was, if I recall correctly, in 1959 when I had the misfortune to be relaxing in the staff room when the rather unpleasant man who used to take lower school Physics and Chemistry reported ill and I was ordered into the breach. Since then I have always spent my free periods in a distant corner of our modest library or strolling into town with Mr Crimson our head of Geography for a cup of coffee in the Copper Kettle Tea Rooms. So I fear that the impact of my positively refusing to deputize for other teachers is bound to be very limited indeed.

Similarly with lunchtime supervision: for many years I have suffered from a rare gastric condition which precludes my being present whilst hordes of ill-mannered school boys (and now girls as well) eat their food. The succession of headmasters at Ridley Road have understood this and have excused my presence in school over the mid-day break. In return I have always taken it upon myself to keep a look-out for any boy who, in defiance of the school rules, strays into any of the charming public houses in our neighbourhood.

Nor can I withdraw from taking games. The recurring problem I have with my knee as the result of an injury sustained during a period of National Service at Catterick has meant I have been let off that particular torture from my very entry into the world of education.

I do not run any clubs or societies after school hours. Or indeed during school hours -- can one do that? Instead of teaching proper lessons, I mean. You also say we should keep our preparation and marking to the barest minimum. My dear chap, it is quite some time since I felt the need to prepare or rather re-prepare my lessons. What was good enough ten years ago and indeed twenty years ago, I feel, is good enough today. Marking pupil's work I have never found to be a burden as it nicely fills the time in those lessons when the class are doing questions from the textbook. It has certainly never crossed my mind to take exercise books home with me.

You make it clear that for the moment all teachers should leave school at 4 o'clock on the dot. But I take it there would be no objection to my continuing to leave at 3.30 on Mondays, Thursdays and Fridays as by special arrangement my free periods come at the end of the day and I am able to catch an early train home.

That leaves your final three instructions: (1) Not to attend any Parent Teacher Association meetings. This I am happy to comply with. I have never liked meeting parents who seem to think that one has nothing better to do with one's evenings but hang around listening to their complaints. Over the years I have managed to avoid a number of parents' evenings by pleading domestic obligations, family commitments and the like but I do remember that at the last such meeting I attended I was forced to listen to the very ill-thought-out views of one boy's father on Harold Wilson cancelling the TSR2. Quite what that had to do with his son's 'O' level prospects I still utterly fail to understand.

(2) To have nothing to do with school plays. This instruction is welcome news indeed as it saves me from the annual chore of devising an excuse for missing the Gilbert & Sullivan operetta that one of my younger colleagues is so anxious to organize every year. I fear he is not an N.U.T. member so the production will perhaps go ahead but wild horses could not get me to watch it if to do so would offend union policy.

(3) Not to go on any school outings. In general I would give my whole-hearted support to this policy (and not just when we are in dispute) but I do every June take a select party of 6th Formers to the Lake District. Indeed my volunteering for such onerous work, albeit during term time, has always been regarded as a major contribution to the life of the school in return for which I am entitled to miss morning assembly and therefore arrive at 9.30 a.m. (and so catch a later train). I would be reluctant to give up these trips as they are highly educational. The boys spend a fortnight in the beautiful English countryside revising for their 'A' levels while I renew my acquaintance with Mrs Cauldicott, the very pleasant widow who keeps the guest house where I always find the warmest of welcomes. I hope I will not in any way be regarded as scab-legging if I do continue this annual trip out of a concern for the pupils in my care.

As you will understand, your list of instructions is all but superfluous. Where duties are voluntary, I simply do not usually volunteer. I should imagine this goes for the majority of teachers at this school. And every other school too, if they have got any sense. Notwithstanding that, I can assure you I whole-heartedly support the union's campaign to bring teachers' pay up to a level consistent with the high level of skill, care and dedication we bring to the practice of this most important profession. Other than that, all I can say is roll on the summer holidays!

Yours sincerely,

Thomas Morgan

AN UNPRECEDENTED OFFER

DEWPEW KITCHENS

Buy a new **DEWPEW** Kitchen and we will give you a **FREE** OVEN! **FREE** HOB UNIT! **FREE** DISHWASHER! **FREE** EXTRACTOR FAN! **FREE** REFRIGERATOR! **FREE** £1000 HOLIDAY FOR TWO! In addition to this SENSATIONAL OFFER there is NOTHING TO PAY FOR TWO YEARS and if you order your new **DEWPEW** Kitchen before April 23 next we will reduce the price by 75%! How can we afford to offer you such a FABULOUS deal? SIMPLE. Our kitchen units are grossly overpriced. You could buy the same quality units elsewhere for a **FRACTION OF THE PRICE!** Why are our kitchen units so grossly overpriced? Because we have to build into their price the cost of all the **FREE** APPLIANCES we will be giving you with your new kitchen and the cost of all our EXPENSIVE ADVERTISING in GLOSSY MAGAZINES and COLOUR SUPPLEMENTS. Why not dispense with the **FREE** APPLIANCES and GLOSSY ADVERTISING and sell the kitchen units at a fair price? Because most people still believe that they can get SOMETHING FOR NOTHING! This statement is AMAZING BUT TRUE! Our research shows that the vast majority of people are gullible and will respond positively to adverts like this. YOU are one of these people. We can say that with the greatest confidence because if you weren't gullible you would have stopped reading this advert long ago. In fact if you are still reading it, despite **DEWPEW** Kitchens admitting that their kitchen units are grossly overpriced and making it clear to you that you won't be getting SOMETHING FOR NOTHING, you are more than gullible, you are a stupid twat! So don't delay, phone **FREE**phone 0900-444-888 and one of our consultants will be round at your house to bullshit you something awful and con you into buying a new **DEWPEW** Kitchen before you can say **FREE** WASHING MACHINE! . . . . because that is what you will be getting along with the other **FREE** APPLIANCES, plus **FREE** TOASTER! **FREE** KETTLE!! **FREE** COFFEEMAKER!!! **FREE** PARKING!!!! **FREE** EXCLAMATION MARKS!!!!! **FREE** NELSON MANDELA!!!!!! (The free Nelson Mandela is a beautiful 6 inch high black figurine which will look lovely on one of the shelves of your new **DEWPEW** Kitchen.) So DON'T DELAY, fill in the coupon **NOW!**

STOCK CLEARANCE!

Save a further 20%

Simply rip out this advertisement and flush it down the toilet.

Black to the drawing-board, lads.

I.Q. OF 140

AND CAN'T REMEMBER?

It's a real problem isn't it? Someone asks you for your **I.Q.** And you can't recall what it is. Or what **I.Q.** stands for. Or whether it's of any significance anyway. I mean look at that Jimmy Savile. He's supposed to have an **I.Q.** of about 200 and all he does is introduce out-of-date records on Sunday lunchtimes. He never says anything intelligent, witty or remotely worth listening to. What are all his **I.Q.**'s doing inside his head? Or then again Ronald Reagan. If he didn't have an autocue he would have been written off as educationally sub-normal years ago. Nobody can convince me his **I.Q.** is even into double figures. And yet I am only a self-opinionated humorist and he is the most powerful man in the world. Makes you think, doesn't it? Even if it doesn't make Ronald Reagan think. Well you probably imagine I am trying to sell you something and *you are right*. It's a little book called *How to improve your memory*. I don't know why I bother really because if I convince you you need it you're *bound* to forget to send off for it. Of course I could try selling my book in the shops but then you might browse through it, developing a photographic memory and not need to buy it.

So here goes. *Rush £10 to me at the following address.* Hang on I've got it here somewhere, on a bit of paper. . .

WHERE WERE THEY ONCE?

An Historical Map of Elton John's Head

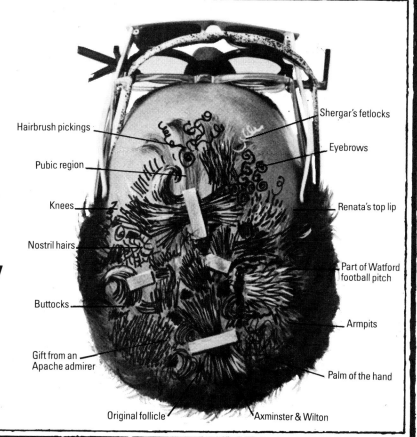

Hairbrush pickings
Pubic region
Knees
Nostril hairs
Buttocks
Gift from an Apache admirer
Original follicle

Shergar's fetlocks
Eyebrows
Renata's top lip
Part of Watford football pitch
Armpits
Palm of the hand
Axminster & Wilton

These fabulous gifts are FREE when you join Sid and Nobby's
WINO CLUB

Sid and Nobby Britain in the one trip are two of the country's leading winos. Sid (left) staggered for 1984 Wino Olympics. Nobby (right) emptied 93 carriages in round the Circle Line. We are proud to offer you this unique opportunity to join their fabulous Wino Club. Membership is open to anyone over 18 who is too smashed to apply.

Gallon can of Gastrol 5 St

Stripped pine Wino Rack. Stacks up to six Winos in comfort.

Haute gutture Winobelt. Made from Parisian string.

Beard totally forked? The Wino Beard Bra lifts and separates.

NOBBY

"Hello there, winos, how are ya, y'all right, I'm all right, I'm OK, I'm all right, y'know, I'm not too bad, me, I'm OK, how you going, don't you worry about me, I'll be all right, I'm right as rain, don't you worry, I'm all right. Bye."

SID

"Tell 'em about the bloody club, you daft old booger."

NOBBY

"Right you are there, Sid, now see here mates, you just send me 30p for your club membership, see, and that'll do me nicely, for me bus fare, see, down to the library, it's lovely and warm in there, see, don't you worry, they got the newspapers see, for me bundle, I can pop them newspapers inside me coat when the lady's not looking, it wasn't me, sir, no, sir, honest, copper, I never touched them newspapers, you got the wrong man, your Worship, you must be blind, with respect . . ."

SID

"Don't listen to him, winos, he's out of his mind he is, you listen to your old mate Sid, now you just send me 30p a month and you'll be getting all these free gifts, for nothing like, from our Club, see, and I'll not be spending it on drink, oh no, 'tis the piss of the Devil, drink, oh yes, I'll be putting it straight in the building society. Cos I could do with a new pair of cider, see. SHOES! New pair of shoes, yes. Fokk. Excuse me now, here comes a passer-by, when you're smiling, when you're smiling, the whole world, excuse me have you got leeurrgh oh booger I sicked up all over him."

Please enrol me as a Lifetime Member of SID AND NOBBY'S WINO CLUB, that'll do me fine.

I enclose cheque/PO for 30p as my first monthly payment or charge my Access/Visa no.
Name...
Bench ....
Thumbprint...
Please send me the *Wino Club Newsletter* every month until I have built up a complete blanket.
I understand that membership of the WINO CLUB commits me to an institution within 28 days god bless you.

Fishing for fag-ends in Filey? Scrabbling for skate in Skegness? The Good Bin Guide sniffs out the gourmet garbage.

Send to: SID AND NOBBY'S WINO CLUB, The Pavement, Camden Town Fruit & Veg. Market, Inverness Street, London NW1, Sir

7

The Young Lady from Bude

There was a young lady from Bude,
Who lived in a town called Bude,
She walked around Bude,
And had a house in Bude,
That silly young lady from Bude.
Where is Bude anyway?

The Iggly Biggly Bog

In the land of the treacle pudding,
Where the crumbly bumbly dwells,
There once was a diddely dooh,
Dee dum dee dum, dee bumm, bum, bum, ta ra,
Ick nock, barble, blick, hic.

The Pussy and the Teapot

Oh pussy oh pussy oh pussy!
Oh tea pot, oh tea pot, oh tea pot!
Oh pussy, oh pussy, oh pussy!
Oh tea pot, oh tea pot, oh tea pot!
Oh pussy, oh pussy, oh pussy!
Oh tea pot, oh tea pot, oh tea pot!
This is quite good stuff this isn't it?
Oh pussy, oh pussy oh bollocks

Yet Another Irritating Limerick

There once was a limerick by me,
That didn't rhyme at all,
It didn't have those two middle lines
which are shorter than the others,
Or scansion at all
That limerick by me.
And it had one line too many.

———•○•———

BBC.
WE HAVE MICHAEL GRADE. YOUR CONTROLLER UNLESS YOU LEAVE A MILLION POUNDS IN A WASTE PAPER BASKET IN KING'S CROSS BY THE WEEKEND YOU WILL NEVER SEE HIM AGAIN.

BBC tv

BRITISH BROADCASTING CORPORATI
TELEVISION CENTRE WOOD LANE LONDON W12 7
TELEPHONE 01-743 8000 TELEX: 265

11th January 1987

cc Head of Security
H.L.E.T.V.
Assistant to the D. G.
Director of Personnel (TV)

Dear Sir,

Thank you for your most interesting ransom note. We are always happy to receive unsolicited material here at the BBC.

May I first of all apologize for the delay in replying? Unfortunately your demand was sent to Artiste's Booking (Variety) by mistake.

It has now been passed to the appropriate department for further perusal.

If you still have Mr. Grade could you pass him the whole department's best wishes. We have of course noticed his absence in the last few months but assumed he must have decided to stay for a further week or so at the Roumanian Television Festival. (Hai Oktai T.V.)

Yours faithfully,

Howard Gilman

Howard Gilman.
(Assistant to the Controller BBC 1)

BBC. A MILLION POUNDS IN THE WASTE PAPER BASKET BY THURSDAY OR ELSE.

BBC tv

BRITISH BROADCASTING CORPORATI
TELEVISION CENTRE WOOD LANE LONDON W12 7
TELEPHONE 01-743 8000 TELEX: 265

17th March 1987

cc Head of Security
H.L.E.T.V.
Assistant to the D. G.
Head of Carpets (TV)
Editor ''Points of View''
Director of Personnel (TV)
Head of Artistes Booking (Variety)
Head of Artistes Booking (Drama)
Head of Artistes Booking (Weather)
Head of Foreign Liaison Radio
I.K.T.P. (Manchester)

Dear Sir,

Once again apologies for the delay. Your letter was sent to ''Points of View'' by mistake. You may have seen the more interesting bits irreverently mocked by Barry Took on Thursday. As I explained before, your demand is currently under active consideration. I am bound to warn you, however, that the figure you mention is rather outside our usual budget for this sort of project.

If we had a million pounds to throw in the rubbish bin we would probably commission another series of the Borgias.

Incidentally, have you approached the Commercial network? I understand Mr. Grade had some connection with Thames T.V. in the past.

Yours faithfully,

Howard Gilman

Howard Gilman.
(Acting Controller BBC 1)

BBC tv

BRITISH BROADCASTING CORPORATION
TELEVISION CENTRE WOOD LANE LONDON W12 7RJ
TELEPHONE 01-743 8000 TELEX: 265781

2nd June 1987

Dear Sir,

May I first of all apologize for the delay in replying? Your ear was sent to Radio Three by mistake. It has now been passed to Dr. Jonathan Miller for further examination. I am sorry to have to take a strong line here, but you are obviously unaware of the way in which a public corporation like the BBC handles its affairs. We simply cannot rush into things, ear or no ear.

Perhaps you would like to come to the centre and see how a programme is made? Tickets are currently available for the following shows; "Wogan on Monday," "Wogan on Tuesday," "Wogan on Wednesday" and a pilot programme which I have myself instituted as part of a new broom sweeping through this department, "Wogan on Friday, Saturday and Sunday." Alternatively, there is a new Situation Comedy, "Coo, Aunty Baggins" starring Molly Sugden and Ian McKellen.

I would also like to point out that one ear is really not sufficient for us to make a judgement in this matter. Would it be possible to send us any other bits of the Grade body in order to assist us?

Thanking you in anticipation.

Yours faithfully,

Howard Gilman

Howard Gilman.
(Controller BBC 1)

Enc. Receipt for one ear for your info. and records.

cc CR 3
H.L.E.T.V.
Director of Personnel (TV)
Assistant to the D. G.
Head of Carpets (TV)
Head of Water Jugs and Glasses, Current Affairs (TV)
Editor "Points of View"
Head of Artistes Booking (Variety)
Head of Artistes Booking (Drama)
Head of Medical Broadcasting (Weather)
I.K.T.P. (Manchester)
I.U.D. (Porthcawl)
Assistant to the Controller, Car Park Allocation (Scotland)
Managing Director, Stationery Supplies (Loose-leaf)
Acting Regional Head of BBC Insignia (Lorries)
Head of Foreign Liaison (Radio)
Head of luxuriant silver hair

c CR 3
H.L.E.T.V.
Director of Personnel (TV)
Assistant to the D. G.
Head of Carpets (TV)
Head of Water Jugs and Glasses, Current Affairs (TV)
Editor "Points of View"
Head of Artistes Booking (Variety)
Head of Artistes Booking (Drama)
Head of Artistes Booking (Weather)
Head of Medical Broadcasting (Southern England)
I.K.T.P. (Manchester)
I.U.D. (Porthcawl)
Assistant to the Controller, Car Park Allocation (Scotland)
Managing Director, Stationery Supplies (Loose-leaf)
Acting Regional Head of BBC Insignia (Lorries)
Head of luxuriant silver hair
Assistant Controller, Roped Enclosures (BBC Foyers)
Managing Director, Light Entertainment (Open University)
GV (Merseyside)
ead of Biros (Enterprises)
ead of Future Appointments (Local Radio)
eputy Head of Future Appointments (Local Radio)
ssistant to the Deputy Head of Future Appointments (Local Radio)
armac Supervisor (Outside Broadcasts)
ontroller of Window Boxes (Caversham)
ting Head of Titles Designate (TV)
naging Director Personalized Number Plates (Local Radio)
ntroller of Eyebrows
B.H.

BBC tv

BRITISH BROADCASTING CORPORATION
TELEVISION CENTRE WOOD LANE LONDON W12 7F
TELEPHONE 01-743 8000 TELEX: 26578

4th November 1987

Dear Sir,

My apologies for the delay in replying. Your letter was sent to Artiste's Booking by mistake.

I have looked, with interest, at what has been satisfactorily identified as a nose, part of an upper lip, a fourth finger (with signet ring belonging to Michael Grade) and a foot (with grey Gucci shoe, belonging to Bill Cotton). Unfortunately I am unable to trace the correspondence relating to this matter. As you are no doubt aware, Mr. Gilman has recently been made Director General and we are in a bit of a pickle here. I can tell you, however, that it would be impossible for a payment of this sort to be made within this financial year. We will keep your request on file until next April.

In the meantime, if you are in financial difficulties, can I remind you that many people find it convenient to spread their payment of the T.V. Licence by buying T.V. Licence Stamps?

Yours faithfully,

Julian Grade

Julian Grade.
(Controller Designate BBC 1)

SO LONG –
and thanks for all the for all the advance...

DOUGLAS ADAMS

The Sequel To
'ABSOLUTELY THE LAST'
Hitch-hiker's Book

FROM THE HITCH-HIKER'S GUIDE TO THE GALAXY:

'Far out in the uncharted backwaters of the unfashionable end of the
Western Spiral arm of the Galaxy lies a small unregarded yellow sun.'

Recognize it! You will.
This opening paragraph — yes, PARAGRAPH — made publishing history!
So fantastic were the sales of the book that the ape-descended life-form
that wrote it was persuaded to do it again. Yes. Douglas Adams wrote
out exactly the same paragraph to begin his next book. And, incredibly,
it worked!
The people of Earth gave him enough little pieces of green paper to buy as
many digital watches as he could possibly want. But still the life-
descended ape-form publishers were not happy.
Which was odd.
Because Douglas was delirious.
They persuaded him to have another go.
And he did it again!
He wrote out exactly the same paragraph, word for word, and the next
one, and a few others from other places in the book and held his breath.
And still the people of Earth gave him little green pieces of paper, except
they were blue now — the green pieces of paper had been abolished
(although Douglas hadn't noticed).

And now, two thousand hours after they nailed a man to his typewriter
for thinking those pieces of paper were a pretty neat idea,
here it is again!
At the beginning of the book!
Only this time Douglas has discovered w i d e s p a c i n g
and it takes up a whole page.

So DON'T PANIC — here it is.
Nearly twenty pages of positively the last Hitch-hiker's Book.
For a while.

A doorstop it ain't.
But the ape-descended life-forms who read this sort of stuff prefer it
that way.

About the Author:
Douglas Adams is not married, has no children,
and still doesn't live in Surrey.
He does, however, have a Porsche, and a Golf
GTi Cabriolet, both of which are equipped with
car-phones. He has a dozen computers, an
enormous hi-fi, a flat in Islington, a house in
Islington, an apartment in New York, and a top
literary agent.

He likes to be seen around town in the company
of someone who once played trumpet for Paul
McCartney and the least memorable one of
'the Pythons'. He is positively obsessive about
expensive restaurants. He is currently
negotiating to buy yet another premises in
Islington where he can go and write.
He is very tall.

HAMLET

LOUIS BENJIMARSH PRESENTS

A Gala Performance
for
Lord O'Lovey of Cottesloe

JULIUS CAESAR

On the Occasion of his 150th Birthday

A LAST-DITCH ATTEMPT TO GET HIM TO RETIRE

IN THE PRESENCE OF *A Peter Hallogram* LORD O'LOVEY HIMSELF

... The Stars Pay Tribute ...

YOU PAY FOR YOUR SEAT

LENA ZAVARONI ✳ LEGGS AND CO. ✳ THE KRANKIES ✳ THE JOHNNY MANN SINGERS
HOWARD KEEL ✳ PAM AYRES ✳ KENNY LYNCH ✳ GARRY WILMOT ✳ BEN ELTON
AND A FEW OTHERS OF WHOM THE DEAR GREAT MAN HAS NEVER HEARD

THE ENTERTAINER

MR PUFF

BOYS FROM BRAZIL

OTHELLO

HENRY V

RICHARD III

MARATHON MAN

KING LEAR

THE HALLOGRAM —
MORE LIFE-LIKE THAN THE REAL THING

✳

SIR PETER HALL

Peter Hall writes:

(ACTUALLY HE DOESN'T WRITE, HE DIRECTS, WHICH IS MUCH EASIER AND BETTER PAID):
I REMEMBER I WAS DIRECTING A PRODUCTION AT GLYNDEBOURNE, A COUPLE OF PRODUCTIONS
AT THE NATIONAL, A COMMERCIAL FOR SOME MARGARINE, A QUICKIE REVIVAL ON BROADWAY
AND ATTEMPTING TO GET MY DIARIES PUBLISHED (MEANWHILE CAMPAIGNING FOR HIGHER GOV-
ERNMENT SUBSIDIES FOR THE ARTS) WHEN SOMEBODY MENTIONED THAT A GALA IN AID OF OLD
LARRYBAGS MIGHT BE A GOOD IDEA...

All Proceeds to:

DAME ANNA NEAGLE'S RETIREMENT HOME FOR CLAPPED-OUT VARIETY ARTISTES,
TEENIE WEENIE ICKY WICKY KIDDIE WINKIES BENEVOLENT FUND,
THE ARTS COUNCIL, AND OTHER CHARITIES

The Anglo-Saxon Chronicle

incorporating the Wessex Advertiser

No. 39 TUESDAY OCTOBER 2ND 1066

1½ GROATS

RAPE & PILLAGE RATE SOARS

by our crime correspondent HUGH ANDCRY

Shock statistics just released reveal the extent of the crime wave which is sweeping the country. In the years 960-1015 (the latest period for which figures are available) there was a 900% increase in the number of recorded rapes and a similar rise in the rate of pillage, burning, looting and monastery sacking.

But in a speech to the Witan the junior Earl responsible for keeping the King's peace said the apparent increase could be due to people being readier to come forward and report such crimes. At least they were when they were still alive. He also dismissed as 'racist' the suggestion that there was any link between the increase in crimes of violence and the numbers of Vikings and Norsemen settling in Northumberland, Mercia, Kent, and anywhere else they could get their hands on.

He said there was no chance of Britain entering a new Dark Age because it had not left the old one yet.

King Cnut: apology

We apologise for the typographical errors which meant that the name Cnut was misspelt throughout the Chronicle's obituary of the late King. Any offence caused by the unfortunate transpositioning of the letters in the name is very much regretted. It was caused by teething troubles at our new manuscript illuminating plant at Wapping and one particularly stupid member of staff who has now been sacked.
Stupid cnut.

WENCH OF THE WEEK

14-year-old Edith Guthriggson

has given up her early ambition to enter a nunnery in Shropshire to become a wimple model in Londontown. And nun too soon, eh lads? Edith has worked already in Winchester and York and hopes to travel abroad, possibly in the Holy Roman Empire. She is certainly someone we would be prepared to go a few leagues with!

RECORD BOOK ADVANCE

A record advance of the whole of the country's wealth is alleged to have been promised to Duke William of Normandy for the rights in his new 'Domesday Book' due to be published as soon as he has usurped the crown.

Publishers of the Bible, Collins, said:

GODWINSON SLAMS FIXTURE PILE-UP:

KING HAROLD GODWINSON last night lashed out at the fixture snarl-up which threatens the England team's chances when they take on the Norman French at Hastings later this month.

The gruelling battle the team fought with the Norwegians at Stamford Bridge on the 21st September leaves Godwinson with injuries to several key members of his squad.

'The whole thing's crazy,' said Godwinson. 'At Stamford Bridge the boys done wonderful. Afterwards we were over the comet. But how can we build up our national side playing so many battles in a season? The Normans have had their squad together for months now, yet we are supposed to get together in a few days.

Frankly I am as sick as a parrot, whatever that is.'

ON OTHER PAGES

Plus!!

Hors d'Oeuvres

Table with View of Tracy Ullman
avec son coulis de tomates
£3.75

Table from Where if Neck is Really Craned
you can just see Melvyn Bragg's agent's back à moutarde
£3.25

Table with Back to Andrew Ridgeley
à l'épinard
£3.25

Table within Headjerking Distance
*of the front entrance near enough to catch the swish
of the revolving door and the Chanel No. 17
wafting in from the street vichyssoise*
£2.90

Table within Earshot of Nigel Dempster
à vinaigre de framboise
£3.75

Seat Still Warm from Simon Le Bon's Bottom
à finocchio
£4.10

Entrées

Table Two Tables Away from Anna Ford
*so that if your dinner partners shut up talking you can just hear her discussing her next
thought-provoking seminal work on the history of something but she hasn't quite decided
yet it depends on the publisher she's with at the moment à dauphinoise*
£10.75

Table Still Bearing Debris
*of Peter Langan's regurgitating his stuffed quail, a dozen oysters and a bottle and a half of claret
over some hapless Sunday supplement interviewer who thought this would be just
another nice, quiet, cushy lunchtime assignment au basilic*
£11.30

Table within Fall-Out Range
*of party of twenty-six Channel Four technicians filming 'Take Six Cooks' on yet another freebie,
flicking their profiteroles and belching on their Chablis while they bemoan their lot and
rail on about overtime and expenses as they guzzle their way round the restaurants
of England for yet another series aux champignons*
£14.95

Assiette Surprise (MIN 2 PERS)
*Seeing Michael Caine actually putting in a personal appearance to collect his annual rake-off
saying he'd miles prefer to be living in the country of his Cockney roots
but just has to be back in LA first thing tomorrow morning for the
usual boring tax reasons you know darling sauce chocolat*
£22.50

Langhams Brassière ~ Hatton Street, Piccadilly. Telephone: 01-223 1443

"THE HEDGEHOG"

TRANSCRIPT OF PRESS BRIEFING BY POLICE SUPERINTENDENT JOHN RUSHNOT AND HIS ASSISTANT DETECTIVE CONSTABLE RON BACKHANDER IN SCOTLAND YARD PRESSROOM. BOTH OFFICERS ARE SEATED, D.C. BACKHANDER ON A FOLDING CHAIR, SUPERINTENDENT RUSHNOT ON HIS FAT ARSE.

SUP: Gentlemen, I would like to brief you as to the latest developments in the hunt for the killer at large in the Suffolk region.

→ What's the difference?

AT THIS POINT D.C. BACKHANDER WHISPERS SOMETHING TO THE SUPERINTENDENT.

→ The Sussex region. Four hundred top police officers working day and night for the last two weeks have finally come up with... a nickname for the killer.

SPORADIC APPLAUSE FROM THE LEFTIE JOURNALISTS.

We shall be calling him 'The Hedgehog'.

PRESS: Why 'The Hedgehog'?

SUP: Because all the nasty wild animals... fox, snake, rat and wolf... have already been used. *Badger?*

PRESS: Is it true that most policemen are of abnormally low intelligence? *Misleading question!*

SUP: I'm sorry... I don't understand the question. Now the attacks have followed a strict pattern. All the victims have been girls.

D.C. BACKHANDER INTERRUPTS TO WHISPER.

Or boys. And they have taken place at night.

ANOTHER WHISPER FROM D.C. BACKHANDER.

And during the day.

PRESS: What is the capital of France?

SUP: We'll have one of our experts look into that immediately. All my top officers are searching every square inch of Hampshire.

PRESS: Why not Sussex? Where the attacks took place.

SUP: You must be joking! There's a mad killer on the loose in Sussex. Besides, we're far too busy in Hampshire now. In addition to extra manpower we have introduced new 3-litre squad cars that make that American cop car noise, you know, WEEEEEEE eeeeeee EEEEEEE eeeeeee EEEEEEE eee like on 'Kojak'. These cars replace the old style car that went 'na na na na nana nana nana nana'.

AT THIS POINT AN OFFICER ENTERED PRESSROOM AND HANDED PIECE OF PAPER TO SUPERINTENDENT.

Ladies and gentlemen, some information has just come in. The Capital of France is Paris.
Now one of the most important clues so far was received yesterday at operational headquarters. A cassette tape with this note; which I will now read.

THE SUPERINTENDENT THEN READS NOTE.

Right, I've read it.

PRESS: Can you read it out loud?

SUP: Alright alright. Have you been drinking? It says "Dear Cops, you still haven't caught me yet." This was in fact a piece of information already known to the police. "Perhaps this tape might help you. Yours, Death-hawk."

PRESS: Death-hawk? *No such animal! I still prefer BADGER.*

SUP: Er... yes. This tape came after we'd already chosen the nickname. We'd have had to reprogramme the computer.

PRESS: Is it true that the police beat up homosexuals and blacks indiscriminately?

SUP: It depends how many men are available. Now this is what was on the cassette. *GOOD POINT*

THE SUPERINTENDENT PLAYED THE CASSETTE WHICH WAS A VERSION OF "WAKE ME UP BEFORE YOU GO-GO" BY "WHAM".

PRESS: That's Wham!

SUP: We've pulled in two gentlemen for questioning. Both rather seedy looking characters, one of them a Greek or something.

PRESS: One eyewitness said the attacker was six foot three.

SUP: That is correct.

PRESS: And another eyewitness said he was only four foot eleven. *NO GAGS WHILE ON DUTY! →*

SUP: Don't worry. My men are searching high and low.

PRESS: Is it not true that a senior police officer has met the killer and spoken to him face to face?

SUP: Yes. So what?

PRESS: Then why wasn't he caught?

SUP: We couldn't nab him. He's a mason. Right, that's all, gentlemen.

THE SUPERINTENDENT THEN GOT UP TO LEAVE AND LOOKED DIRECTLY AT ME.

SUP: 'Ere, Constable, there's a bloke down there writing all this down. Quick get him!

AT THIS POINT TWO POLICE OFFICERS CAME TOWARDS ME AND

Well done, Super! Find out Hedgehog's address. I want to invite him round for supper. — Commissioner

SUPPLEMENT TO "POLICE v. PRESS (HEDGEHOG)"

MAP SHOWING LOCATION OF ATTACKS
Notice how the locations of crimes conform to set patterns:
1. None of the attacks took place in the sea.
2. The attacks all seem to take place wherever there's a red dot. We're going to put a red dot on Scotland Yard and nab the attacker when he turns up.

AN AERIAL PHOTOGRAPH TAKEN AT THE SCENE OF THE LATEST CRIME

THIS MAN IS ARMED AND COULD BE DANGEROUS

PC "Chuckles" Cleaver
(Special Branch)

"THE HEDGEHOG"

THE OTHER PSYCHOS

THE FOX

THE WOLF

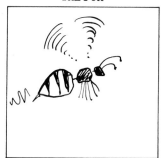

THE WASP

THE HEDGEHOG

The one eyewitness who claims to have actually seen "The Hedgehog" sent us this rough drawing.

POLICE TOP BRASS BLAST PUBLIC

Police chiefs today criticised the general public for not helping their bobbies enough. Speaking at a dinner given in his dining room by his wife, Chief Inspector Dennis Faircop said, 'Our lads are out trying to put "The Hedgehog" behind bars where he belongs. They desperately need the public's help. While they're out fighting crime there's all that washing-up to be done back at the flat, to say nothing of the ironing and the hoovering. A lot of my officers need help with polishing their uniform buttons and doing their shoelaces up. The public CAN help. All they have to do is pop round to their local bobby's house every day. And then there's that difficult detective work, you know, finding out who done what crime. That's really quite a tough task ... and thick coppers can't be expected to do it ... even with the help of Shaw Taylor.

Oh yes. Another thing. If the bleedin' public didn't keep committing crime the police would be able to get on with their regular work, like telling American tourists where Buckingham Palace is and wearing outsize helmets and stick-on nylon moustaches.' The Inspector went on: 'Any more rhubarb crumble, darling?'

JENNIFER'S DIARY

THE CHARITY BALL

After my brief stay in London I went down to Sussex to visit the Hon. Nicholas Bennett-Jones who is presently staying at the Old Snortings Rest Home and Rehabilitation Centre, as a condition of his bail, while he awaits his trial on drug-dealing charges at the Central Criminal Court, Old Bailey. Nicky seemed a little low in spirits but we had some happy laughs when he asked if I had brought him anything and I said: Yes. A bunch of grapes.

From there I went back to London for the Annual Champagne and Caviare Famine Relief Charity Ball at the Grosvenor Lane Hotel. Among those I met in the toilets were... Lady Charlotta de Grenville, Miss Amanda FitzPatrick, Lord Gussie Withers and the Hon. Nicholas Bennett-Jones.

▲ The Marquis of Lamhurst

◀ Samantha FitzWilliams-Faulkner: a quiet moment at the Duke of Cheshire's garden party.

Mr and Mrs Jocelyn Simpson pose for the cameras after their wedding at Marylebone Registry Office. The best man is Aussie Andrews.
▼

by Garard Mellor

Mel Smith

MELVYN *("Mel")* **SMITH** was born on December 3rd 1952 in abject penury. Though fantastically talented he had not a penny to his name. His parents however were extremely well off. His father, a highly intelligent man, was a bookmaker by trade and knew that there is no point in giving money to new-born babies because they eat it. So Mel was several years old before he even owned a Rolls Royce.* On his fourth birthday Mel entered "the business", delighting his parents with a little conjuring trick. (It was crap, actually, but you know what parents are like.) Encouraged by their enthusiasm Mel devoted his life to the theatre. His controversial series of *Nativity Plays (1955-7)* shocked an unready world. These he wrote, devised, directed and starred in, delighting his parents with *The Virgin And The Donkey (1955), Up The Donkey (1956)* and *Un Homme Et Un Donkey (1957).* By 1958 he was ready to leave the cupboard under the stairs and attended the local primary school in London. He smoked very large cigars for his age and soon featured in a number of long-running jokes about his weight including *Hello Fatty (1958), When Did You Last See Me Fatter (1958),* and *Fat Fat Fat Your Nose Is As Long As A Tomato (1959).* Being extremely large Mel found he

Mel, aged 6.

could make people laugh if he told them he'd beat them to pulp if they didn't, and his comedy career was launched. But it was a very different struggle to that of Griff. For a start he did not possess an elk costume. Nor did he have the advantage of being born Hereditary President for Life of The Cambridge Footlights Society. Though his performance as the Head of the Chemistry Department in the Latimer Upper School Revue brought the flattering comment "See me afterwards", his comic talents did not fully emerge until the musical production of *Mother Courage (1962)* where he

Griff Rhys Jones

GRIFFITH *("Griff")* **RHYS JONES** was born on November 6th 1953 in CARDIFF *("Diff").* It is said that, at his birth, wise men stayed in a stable full of shitting animals – more or less anything with a roof being preferable to a Welsh hotel.

The preceding months had been rich with dark portents. A New Zealander had climbed Everest. A golden crown hovered over the head of young Princess Elizabeth for several moments before landing on it. For seventeen years before the event, shepherds in the hills above the city, driving their poor shrivelled pies to market, nightly observed a huge neon finger pointing out of the heavens which read "Bevan's Noted Winkles: often buttered, never bettered." On October 4th, an Angela appeared to Griff's father in a dream and got him all hot and bothered. She announced herself to be "an Assistant Stage Manager sent by Godfrey," and at this she flapped her monstrous set of wings, which then fell over exposing the prompter to the audience.

But the birth itself was largely without incident, apart from being incredibly well reviewed and showered with prestigious awards.

Griff's grandfather on his mother's side, Sir Dylwyn Rhys Whys, was an eminent

man of science. In 1931 he narrowly failed to win the Nobel Prize for his discovery of the miniscule holes in the sides of biros. His paternal grandfather, however, was a humble pharmacist. He sold a patent brand of genital aftershave from a cart in the mines and died in poverty and not inconsiderable discomfort. Little is known about his grandmothers except that they are both alive with active and powerful libel lawyers. Griff's mother and father were Brodwyd Rhys Jones and Llynwyth Rhys Jones, a doctor and a nurse, but not

Griff's granny cringing to The Queen (1953).

played the recorder. Sick at heart at the cruel laughter, Mel determined to leave home and seek a new life in London, where he had heard that the streets were paved with gold. He left by the front door, looked at the streets, went "Tsk" the way one does and went back to bed. Here he stayed up for three nights in a row, this being the kind of man Mel is.

This long and intensely private communion with his wine changed him, and his sheets, forever. On the fourth day, for a bet, he took four A-levels, read Experimental Psychology at Oxford, directed dozens of plays, became a connoisseur of fine champagne and President of the Oxford University Dramatic Society and joined the Royal Court Theatre as Assistant Director. It was a complicated seven-horse accumulator, but it came good and Mel won £750,000. Moments later he lost it again playing "double or quits" – delighting his parents, whom by this time he had driven insane.

Secretaries of Talkback weighing one of Mel's testicles.

Mel threw himself into his work. Plays that he has seen include: *Richard III (1964), The Government Inspector (1964), The Real Inspector Hound (1968), A Day In The Death Of Joe Egg (1967), Love's Labour's Lost (1965), It's A Mad World My Masters (1966), Hamlet (1966), Whoops, Not In My Panties Mr Gisbourne! (1967), Death Of A Salesman (1967), Henry VI Part II (1968), The Homecoming (1968), Waiting For Godot (1969), Two Into One Makes Sex (1969), The Pyjama Cord (1969), Genüg Titties Mit Der Reichsdoktor (1969), Pyjama Bottoms (1969), The Pyjama Game* generally well received, though some critics uncharitably noted that they could not remember, classically speaking, either that the Virgin Mary had been betrothed to an elk, or that an elk had ordered the death of the first born or even that an elk sat on the right hand of God leading community songs and taking outrageously long curtain calls. Nonetheless, Griff was certainly noticed, and by the time he was five he had become the top-earning elk in showbusiness. He saved prudently and by the time he went to school at the age of six he was already a millionaire many times over. He

(1969), The Merry Arseholes Of Windsor (1970), The Relapse (1970), Pyjama Middles (1970), No Pyjamas Please We're British (1970), Troilus And Cressida (1971), Troilism In Pyjamas (1971), The Royal Hunt Of The Sun (1971), John Bull's Other Island (1972), The Cherry Orchard (1972), Seagulls Over Sorrento (1972), The Pyjamacoming (1972), Pyjamas Over Sorrento (1972), The Pyjama Inspector (1973), The Real Pyjama Inspector (1973), Love's Pyjamas Lost (1973), Waiting For Pyjamas (1973), King Lear (1974), The Revenger's Tragedy (1974), The Revenger's Pyjamas (1974), The Royal Hunt Of The Pyjamas (1974), John Bull's Other Trouser Leg (1975), Othello (1976), Macbeth (1977), Three Sisters (1978), Joseph And His Amazing Technicolour Pyjamas (1979), Twelfth Night (1980), Evita (1982) and *Twelfth Nightie (1983)*. He didn't enjoy any of them. So, after Lindsay Anderson was slightly rude to him (in what has since become known as "The Paper Bag Incident") Mel's chance came. He quit the stage and plunged into the world of advertising where, by earning staggering

Princess Diana vomits into the shrubbery after hearing how many dresses Griff's wife has.

necessarily respectively. His father Brodwyn (or Llynwyth) remembers his son fondly. Which is curious because he doesn't have a son called fondly. Griff is especially good to his mother. She regularly receives money from him, and he writes to her every day pointing out which mantelpieces need dusting and 'Sorry about all the washing up Mrs J.'

Griff's peculiar genius made itself felt early. But this was soon solved by cutting two leg-holes in a plastic bag, and placing his arms through the handles. By the age of two he was talking fluently, exhausting his doting parents by keeping them up all night to go through his next day's lines. At four he made his theatrical debut in the school nativity play, where he appeared, at his own insistence, as an elk. The play was

The shed in Griff's garden.

The funny bit from MORONS FROM OUTER SPACE.

was unusually small for his age, but, happily, he found he could forestall playground bullies by making them laugh. He did this by inserting lit matches under his fingernails, giving himself agonising Chinese burns and stabbing his tiny body repeatedly with a pair of dividers drawing blood and applause. He drew appreciative and loyal bullies from miles around, considerately even buying their tickets for them despite the disgraceful prices charged him by the touts. He was nine when he left hospital and returned to school. He studied hard to compensate: for he was still less than six inches tall. At about this time, Griff's comic talents began to emerge. He entertained neighbours and friends by imitating Peter Sellers, going "Neeeeeeh. Neh," buying gigantic houses

Mel arrives home regularly at 9.30 a.m. every day.

amounts of money, he was able to become much more impressively bankrupt than his career had so far allowed him to do. As well as starring in *Not The Nine O'Clock News* as The Fat One, as Mel in *Alas Smith And Jones*, as The Fat One From Not The Nine O'Clock News in *Muck And Brass* on TV, he has directed three West End productions and been brilliantly mellish in seven movies. But it was his role as Voice of 2nd Giraffe in Talkback Radio's award-winning commercial campaign for Holroyd's Shapelee Beef'n'Onion Balls which really enabled him to achieve his first six-figure

overdraft. His bank manager Mr Loon of the First National Bank of Toytown is delighted with his progress, as are his doctors. The injections are taking root, and as soon as it can be arranged for the right person to die in a 'road accident' and suitable organs spooned out of the mess, Mr Loon should be well on the way to a new identity in Venezuela. Mel, in the meantime, from his office in London's teeming Chinese quarter, delights in his role as Britain's leading international radio tycoon. The company he runs with Griff has won many prestigious awards including The Guinness Book Of Records Trophy for Most Hangers-On In A Single Room, and Mel is there every day from nine in the morning till half-past three in the afternoon the following Thursday. A typical day begins with stocktaking on the company fridge, followed by a series of interviews with his cigar merchant and taking his Mum to the shops. Around mid-morning an inkling may emerge. The writers are summoned. They work through the night painstakingly turning this into a glimmer. About six hours after the deadline, Talkback's staff despatch writer arrives to take this to Los Angeles, returning with a large container truck marked "Swag". This allows the glimmer to be transmuted, as if by

magic, into a concept. From there the process is easy: idea/sensible idea/wastepaper basket/lunch suggestion. Et voilà! In fact, this month Mel has signed a new ten-lunch contract with Twentieth Century Synopses and been voted Best Loved Customer by the Directors and Shareholders of Bollinger et Cie.

As for his private life, Mel doesn't have one. His tiny ex-directory egg-box in London's Bayswater souk, which he shares with his beloved Lyn and 200 friends and business acquaintances, is open all hours. Mel enjoys every bit of his success. He has come a long way from his poverty-stricken beginnings in Chiswick. Far, far more than 3½ miles as the crow flies, he insists. Drop round anytime to The Foyer, 23, Plaza of the Glorious 19th Ottobre, General Malcolm O'Ruiz District, London W11. Please bring a pint of milk.
*Now 32, he has very nearly finished eating it, only the cotter-pins, the rear seat and the huge noisy clock on the dashboard eluding him to date.

The only man in Britain who is funnier than Mel and Griff.

in the country, and sleeping with Swedish models who were after his money. It was this which enabled him to hold his head up in front of his friend Douglas Adams – author of *The Hitchhiker's Guide To The Galaxy* – who was not only richer but over seven and a half feet taller, while they were contemporaries at Brentwood School in Essex, England. Thence to Emmanuel College, Cambridge, where Griff read English and History and drank a fantastic amount of lager. He was pissed for eight years, enabling him to become a BBC Light Entertainment Producer under the famed

Prince Charles' famous impression of Griff.

David Hatch – himself the shortest Head of Department in the organisation's history. Here Griff produced a series of brilliant and innovative radio programmes including *Brain Of Britain*, *Top Of The Form* etc.

In his spare time he and Douglas Adams worked as bodyguards for a group of sinister terrorists whom they believed to be Arab princes, but who later turned out to be Jimmy Mulville and Rory McGrath who were also drunk but not actually blind drunk and dribbling on their ties. By the end of 1978 Griff had frittered away his fortune, and dressed in baggy Oxfam suits, shirts made from asbestos milk cartons and huge clumpy shoes made by cutting holes in novelty candles. He was desperate for work so he joined *Not The Nine O'Clock News* and became staggeringly rich and famous, acquiring a wife, 2,785 cars, a $15m movie contract, ten houses and the Society of West End Theatre's Award for the Best Comedy Performance of the Year for his portrayal of Lord Fancourt Babberley in *Charley's Aunt (1983)*. From this nightmare he awoke screaming and foreswore lager forever. To this day not one drip of the gnat's fluid has passed his lips. He lives quietly with his wife Jo and son George in Brondesbury, Enfield and Suffolk respectively where he is an antique dealer.

He dresses simply in baggy £900 Gianni Versace suits, shirts made from the soft underside of llamas' scrotums and huge award-winning clumpy shoes designed by Ove Arup and Partners. He writes books, draws brilliant cartoons, directs stunning productions in the theatre, plays the guitar and is a superb cook. In fact he is loathsome in every regard.

Griff Rhys Jones is a director of several companies including INTERNATIONAL JONES HOLDINGS (Franz Joseph Land) Ltd, GRIFFCO S.A., GmBh (1980) Ltd, UNITED RHYS OF SWAZILAND (MINING) Inc., OFFSHORE WALLETBULGE (Europe) Ltd, and the SHADY group of companies. All inquiries and offers of money to: TRANSWORLD GEORGE RHYS JONES INVESTMENTS S.A., The Governor's Mansion, Grand Cayman, Cayman Islands, P.O.24, Zurich.